Budgetary Control in Academic Libraries

**FOUNDATIONS IN LIBRARY
AND INFORMATION SCIENCE   VOLUME 5.**

Editors: Hans H. Weber, Assistant Director for Technical Services
  University of Houston Libraries, Houston
  Warren N. Boes, Director of Libraries
  University of Georgia Libraries, Athens

FOUNDATIONS IN LIBRARY AND INFORMATION SCIENCE

A Series of Monographs

    SERIES EDITORS: HANS H. WEBER, Assistant Director for Technical Services, University of Houston Libraries, Houston

    WARREN N. BOES, Director of Libraries, University of Georgia Libraries, Athens

Volume 1. THE MEXICAN AMERICAN:
A Critical Guide to Research Aids
BARBARA J. ROBINSON, Bibliographer for Latin American and Mexican American Studies, University of California Library, Riverside, and *J. CORDELL ROBINSON,* Associate Professor, Department of History, California State College, San Bernardino

Volume 2. A PRACTICAL APPROACH TO SERIALS CATALOGING
LYNN S. SMITH, Head, Serials Dapartment, University of California Library, Riverside

Volume 3. THE MICROFORM REVOLUTION IN LIBRARIES
MICHAEL R. GABRIEL, Coordinator of Government Publications, Microforms and Serials, Mankato State University Library, and *WILLIAM C. ROSELLE,* Director University of Wisconsin Library, Milwaukee

Volume 4. CHINA IN BOOKS:
A Basic Bibliography in Western Language
NORMAN E. TANIS, Director, *DAVID L. PERKINS,* Chief Bibliographer and *JUSTINE PINTO,* all California State University Library, Northridge

Volume 5. BUDGETARY CONTROL IN ACADEMIC LIBRARIES
MURRAY S. MARTIN, Associate Dean of Libraries, Pennsylvania State University Library, University Park

Volume 6.   COST ANALYSIS OF LIBRARY FUNCTIONS:
A Total System Approach
BETTY JO MITCHELL, Associate Librarian, *NORMAN E. TANIS,* Director and *JACK JAFFE,* all California State University Library, Northridge

Volume 7.   A GUIDE TO ACADEMIC LIBRARY INSTRUCTION
HANNELORE B. RADER, Center of Educational Resources, Eastern Michigan University, Ypsilanti

Volume 8.   THE MANAGEMENT OF A PUBLIC LIBRARY
HAROLD R. JENKINS, Director, Kansas City Public Library, Kansas City, Missouri

Volume 9.   DEVELOPMENT AND ORGANIZATION OF MEDICAL LIBRARIES
CHARLES W. SARGENT, Director, Texas Tech University Medical Library, Lubbock

Volume 10. COLLECTION DEVELOPMENT IN LIBRARIES
Edited by: *GEORGE B. MILLER, JR.,* Assistant Dean for Collection Development, University of New Mexico Library, Albuquerque and *ROBERT E. STUEART,* Dean, School of Library Science, Simmons College, Boston

Volume 11. INTRODUCTION TO SERIALS MANAGEMENT
Edited by: *SHERE CONNAN,* Serials Librarian, University of California Library, San Diego

The Budgetary Control Cycle

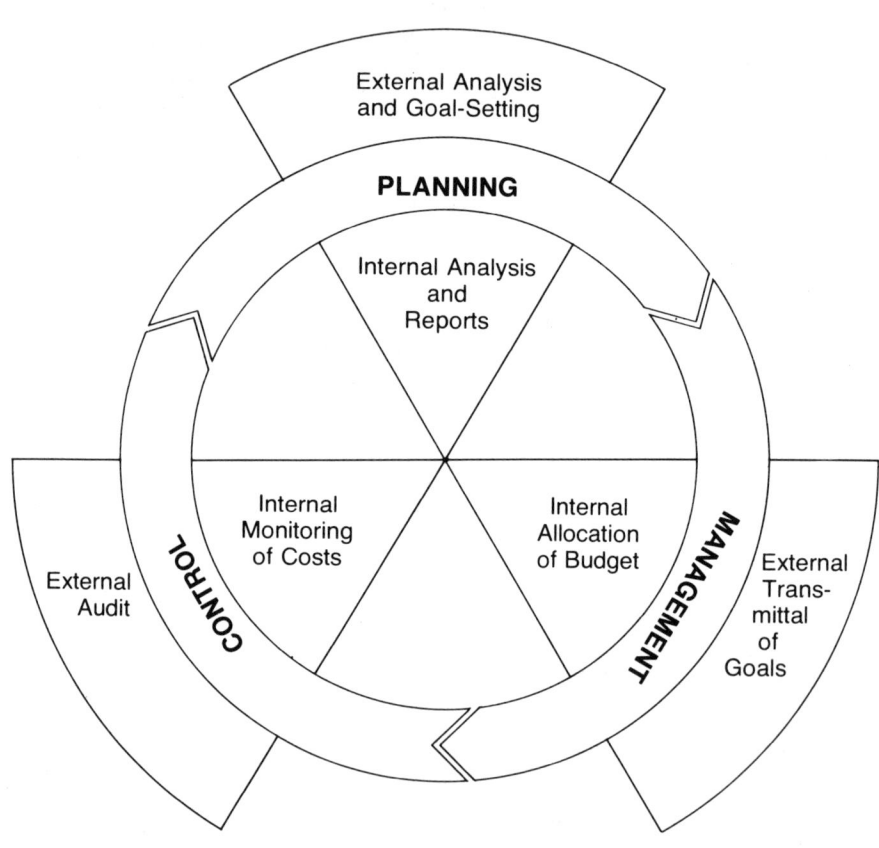

Budgetary Control in Academic Libraries

by MURRAY S. MARTIN
*Associate Dean of Libraries,
Pennsylvania State University,
University Park, Pennsylvania*

 JAI PRESS
Greenwich, Connecticut

Library of Congress Cataloging in Publication Data

Martin, Murray S.
  Budgetary control in academic libraries.

  (Foundations in library and information sciences; v. 5)
  Bibliography: p.
  Includes index.
  1. Libraries, University and college—Finance. 2. Libraries, University and college—Administration. I. Title. II. Series.
  Z675.U5M338   025.1'1   76-5648
  ISBN 0-89232-010-9

Copyright © 1978 by JAI Press
321 Greenwich Avenue
Greenwich, Connecticut 06830
All rights reserved
ISBN: 0-89232-010-9
Library of Congress Catalog Card Number 76-5648
Manufactured in the United States of America

Preface

This book was conceived in response to a suggestion from Herbert Johnson, which might, roughly translated, run, "You are always talking about budgets, why don't you write about them?" After less than mature deliberation, I accepted the challenge. It would be more comfortable to ascribe the impulse to more dignified professional concerns, but, be that as it may, I have tried to put together ideas and insights which could prove helpful to other librarians required to understand and work with the financial side of library operations. It has been a laborious process, and an enjoyable one as well. In the course of my background reading I discovered a book by a man of great good sense who in his concluding statement suggested that perhaps someone might want to write a "how to" book. My endeavor was to provide one such book, and perhaps if it ever comes to his attention Gerald Robins might feel that the result was not unworthy.

There is no pretense that this is a definitive study of budgetary practices, nor that it will answer all the questions that could be asked. Librarianship, for all that it deals with information, ideas and books, is basically a very practical activity. It was therefore surprising to me to find so little written about budgets—and it is my hope that this book will help to fill that void and encourage other librarians to give more consideration to this important matter.

My thanks are due to Warren Boes for his help on editorial and substantive matters, to the members of The Pennsylvania State University Library Staff who have had to live so long with "my book" and to Mrs. Shirley J. Davis who has (with quizzical eyebrow and fingers of steel) typed and retyped what must have seemed an endless succession of pages.

Contents

Preface	vii
Table of Tables	xi
Table of Diagrams	xiii
1. The Need for Fiscal Management	3
2. What Is a Budget	8
3. The Purpose of Budgetary Control	15
4. Preliminary Budget Analysis	24
Analysis of the Budget Request Document	28
Analysis of the Existing Library Budget	31
Personnel-related Expenses	33
Goods and Services	39
Library Materials	43
Reserve or Discretionary Funds	44
Income	45
Summary of Budget Analysis	46
5. Collection of Information in Support of a Budget Request	49
Consultation	58
6. The Use of Statistics to Support a Budget Request	62
7. Budgetary and Economic Restraints and the Setting of Priorities	75
Constraints	80
Priorities	86
Synthesis	90
8. Presentation and Justification of a Budget Request	94

9. Setting up the Budget ... 105
    Personnel-related Expenses ... 107
    Library Materials ... 113
    Goods and Services ... 128
    Discretionary or Reserve Funds ... 133
    The Accounting Structure ... 135
10. Coping with Change ... 137
11. Monitoring the Budget ... 145
    Personnel-related Expenses ... 150
    Library Materials ... 156
    Goods and Services ... 160
    Income ... 163
    The Reporting Function ... 165
12. Closing out the Budget ... 167
13. Retrospect: Important Issues to Remember ... 175

Appendix. The State University Libraries: a Case Study ... 178
Glossary ... 206
References ... 209
Index ... 213

Tables

Table 1.	The Budget of the State University Libraries.	32
Table 2.	Personnel-Related Expenses— Departmental Distribution.	36
Table 3.	Goods and Services.	40
Table 4.	Library Materials Costs.	43
Table 5.	Workload-activity Indicators Used at the Pennsylvania State University.	55
Table 6.	Projection of Activity Indicators.	69
Table 7.	Changes in Reference Services.	72
Table 8.	Changes in the Distribution of Expenditures on Library Materials.	78
Table 9.	The State University Libraries. Summary of the Budget Increase Requests for the Fiscal Year 197–.	103
Table 10.	The State University Libraries. Distribution by Area of the Budget for Library Materials.	121
Table 11.	Straight-line Projection of Periodical Costs.	122
Table 12.	Allocation for Life Sciences.	128
Table 13.	Contingency Fund Record.	134
Table 14.	Adjustments Made to Zero Budget, 1974/75. The Pennsylvania State University Libraries.	141
Table 15.	Projected and Actual Expenditures for the Fiscal Year 197–.	172

Diagrams

The Budgetary Control Cycle		*Frontispiece*
Diagram 1.	Budgetary Relationships within an Institution	11
Diagram 2.	Analysis and Projection of Total Wage Expenditures	38
Diagram 3.	Relationship of Predicated Expenditures to Total Budget	47
Diagram 4.	Trends in Activity Indicators	70
Diagram 5.	Distribution Trends of Expenditures on Library Materials	79
Diagram 6.	Buying Power, Expressed in Units Purchased, of a Static Budget for Library Materials	85

*Budgetary Control
in Academic Libraries*

Chapter 1

The Need for Fiscal Management

> *Budget administration or fiscal management is a year-round occupation; and the procedure of preparing, presenting and negotiating the budget is rapidly becoming a continuum that is likely to begin over a year in advance of the fiscal year to which the budget applies.* (Rogers and Weber, 1961).

When budgets were growing rapidly in the late sixties, good management seemed less necessary than the expansion of programs. Since that time the availability of funds has been reduced and management has become indispensable. Further, demands for public accountability have required institutions of higher education to examine closely all expenditures, both in pursuit of possible savings and in order to ensure that expenditures are indeed made in ways which serve the institution best. Libraries, now that they may no longer rely on ever-increasing financial support, face a situation where the levels of expenditure are being held steady or may even contract. Fiscal management in such circumstances certainly requires the continuous attention suggested by Rogers and Weber.[1]

Other social changes over the last several years have added to the complications by introducing a political element, generally characterized as "participatory management." The sharing of information, the collective nature of many decisions within the library and the need for negotiations with other university units, make most budgetary decisions protracted exercises in diplomacy.

Nevertheless, although the days are past when drawing up a budget was a simple process and its management confined to a few administrators, the need continues for careful analysis of financial requirements and frequent, accurate information on expenditures. The ability to provide such information predicates a knowledge of budgetary control more sophisticated than has usually been available to librarians. This book, which is conceived as being practical rather than theoretical, has been designed to provide a framework on which academic librarians can construct the necessary budgetary procedures. While it is generally concerned with medium- and large-sized academic libraries, the principles stated and the techniques outlined can be applied to other situations.

While policy decisions on services and programs are undoubtedly basic to fiscal decisions, it would require a monumental work to discuss policies on such a level. Where necessary, the effects of such decisions will be discussed in order to clarify the background needed in making financial allocations, but the basic purpose is to concentrate on the process of budget-making and budgetary control as an essential administrative activity. This activity should support and reflect other policy decisions rather than control them; but, without a knowledge of the financial situation, decision-makers can seldom arrive at acceptable conclusions on other activities.

Matters which will be discussed include the development, presentation and control of a library budget. It is recognized that there are specific differences between institutions which cannot be dealt with in a general work. Nevertheless all libraries are in a situation where they have a specific amount of money intended to be spent in certain ways. All, therefore, need to be able to predict, allocate and control expenditures. There is a further need to maintain records in some manner that will enable essential decisions to be made, either at budget-preparation time or in the course of a year when it is discovered that adjustments must be made.

While everyone realizes the difference between being able to ask for extra money (with reasonable expectation of being gratified by the results) and being required to continue operating with the same budget, despite increasing costs, not everyone recognizes the fundamental differences caused in budget management and control by such a change.

It requires the careful examination of existing programs and the evaluation of new ones. The substitution of new programs for old, the changing of priorities, calls for "difficult decisions." "These risk-taking decisions are the responsibility of administrators" who with appropriate advice and consultation "must decide in which areas [the library] can make the greatest impact."[2] Such rearrangements of programs require carefully prepared rearrangements of funding. Raffel is correct when he says:

> Although helpful, an economic analysis of a university (or public) library is insufficient because libraries operate as political systems and thus improving libraries requires political analysis.[3]

Political analysis must, however, continue to be supported by economic analysis or the librarian may be in the embarrassing situation of trying to spend the same dollar twice. Fiscal considerations cannot be the sole determinant in policy-making. Equally, political need cannot be the sole factor considered in library planning, particularly when money itself is in short supply.

Many approaches have been used to help solve the problem, including cost-benefit analysis and the Planning Programming Budgeting System (PPBS), but they are less easily applied to education than to industry or business, principally because the variables are too numerous and the goals much less easily quantifiable than for example the maximization of profits. They nevertheless provide tools whereby the librarian can analyze needs and the practicability of goals. All methods of analysis which are concerned with future possibilities are, of their nature, subject to error because external circumstances are generally not under the control of the analyst.

Librarians must, however, try to predict the future, even if for so simple a purpose as to forestall the overfilling of the shelves in the stacks. Simple as it may seem, it frequently comes as a shock to the librarian or administrator to realize the space expansion requirements imposed by the purchase of a given quantity of materials. To put it in concrete terms, 50,000 books added to a library require at least one mile of shelving. This is a very simple example of the consequences inherent in any one decision, but it could be multiplied and made more complex to reflect the many other programmatic effects of decisions relating to library services.

The budget is a primary tool for use in making such predictions, since everything has a cost and the value to the library of making alternative uses of any given quantity of dollars can be assessed. Similarly, the record of expenditures provides a ready way of determining whether, indeed, the decisions taken are being implemented. This kind of information-gathering is particularly important when there is no longer certainty of access to extra funds. Finally, it helps to identify particular areas of need, thus directing attention to programs that require consideration, whether for reshaping or for redirection of resources.

The very important study of the economics of academic libraries carried out by Baumol and Marcus was completed at the end of the period of rapid growth. As a consequence the comparative statistics and growth patterns which were used to derive support data for financial forecasting are now superseded by new estimates based on the need to survive. The element of comparison is an important one to remember when preparing estimates, and reference to standards derived from comparative statistics is necessary. "Every college and university must keep up with the standards offered by others if it is to obtain students and faculty members of comparable quality."[4] Unfortunately, such comparisons are easier to make and achieve a readier response when funds are easy to obtain. Reference to abstract standards has less impact when money is tight, unless such references are buttressed by very careful analysis of the library's programs and goals in relation to those of the university. When the choice, as it so often must now be, is between programs or between different sizes of reduction, standards tend to lose credibility. An analytical approach which demonstrates the effect of change on services to the institution has much more impact. Such an approach requires detailed knowledge of present expenditures and careful forecasts of the effects of change. These elements require a more intensive approach to fiscal planning than has been usual for libraries in the past. This is a time when libraries are faced with new demands and new needs resulting from the development of new technologies. Libraries' critical evaluation of the benefits gained from such programs and a careful estimate of all costs, both additional and substitutional, are now a regular part of the budget process, adding a dimension not foreseen a decade ago.

Briefly, the various steps in planning and controlling budgets are: the preparation of a budget request based on future needs, the presentation of that budget, the casting of an actual budget after negotiations both with the institution's administration and with the library's own administrators and the monitoring of expenditure during the year. Other activities may be added, such as response to a position freeze, other fiscal action by the institution, or the reexamination of budgetary allocations in the light of newly discovered needs or changes in programs. The frequency with which these events occur is well illustrated in Thomson's survey of community colleges.[5] A glance at most library news journals will make it clear that such actions are not confined to any one kind of library. Even while the library is coping with such crises, preparations for the next year may be under way. In such circumstances budgetary management is a "year-round occupation" which requires the close attention of the library administration.

NOTES
1. Rogers and Weber (1971), p. 89.
2. "Report on Peter Drucker's Speech at ACRL Membership Meeting," submitted by Linda Beaupre, *College and Research Libraries News,* No. 8, September 1975, p. 263.
3. Raffel, p. 312.
4. Baumol and Marcus (1973), p. 40.
5. Thomson (1975), pp. 47–49.

Chapter 2

What Is a Budget?

> *The budget is the central expression of how ... finite resources will be allocated, the terms of the annual cease-fire, as it were ... between the competing claims of different advocates for more money.* (Virginia Held, PPBS Comes to Washington.)

While it is not the intention of this work to explore the political basis of budget-making, it is necessary to be aware of it. Although Virginia Held is describing the budget process in the federal government, her statement[1] may aptly be applied to the development of institutional or state budgets. The budget document records the long process and the many hands which have played a part in its development. As stated by Natchez and Bupp:

> The budget reflects simultaneously a yearly process of administration and decisions among alternative political priorities. That is, budgets are at once measures of the way government is organized and of the policy decisions the organization implements.[2]

In its simplest form a budget may consist of three of four lines which summarize categories of expenditure, and this kind of summary is the one used for transmittal of budget information. It is in a sense a coded statement, the key to which is shared by all financial and budget officers because of their knowledge of the process implicit in the bald statement. The use of that key expands it to a complex planning document as each element is broken down into individual expenditures. Even a long and involved budget, including numerous funds or couched in terms of programs, is merely a representation of what will be done with the allocated sums of money. It is given actuality only by the carrying out of the transactions implicit in the accounts. In this way a budget is both object and process, and this dual nature calls forth a variety of responses, depending on the role that an individual plays in relation to that budget. This is to be expected since budgets, like all policy documents, mean different things to different people. An understanding of these different views is essential for effective budget-making.

First, it is important to place the budget in perspective. As Summers points out:

> We are all to some degree part of an executive budget. The state university library's budget becomes a part of the executive budget of the president. The president's budget becomes, perhaps, a part of the executive budget of the chancellor of higher education, and the chancellor's budget becomes a part of the executive budget of the governor.[3]

We might have extended the chain downward to the section head and upward to the state legislature, but no matter how many levels are included it is easily seen that each level may well hold a completely different view of a particular item or program. While to the librarian the library budget will control the succeeding year's activities, for the governor it is simply a part of one program among the many to which resources must be allocated. Each one consequently views the money involved and the goods and services it will buy from a completely different standpoint, using different measures of value. These differences do not necessarily imply conflict, although that may sometimes be the case. They do, however, imply change, whether it be in format or in priorities. If this is understood, it is easier to live with the results, since these are seldom exactly in line with the intent of the originator of a budget request.

To the library staff the budget represents a kind of control system, something which sets the limits of the resources with which they must seek to achieve their goals. The individual staff member seldom thinks of the budget as a whole, may not indeed think of it at all, except on those occasions when lack of money frustrates a particular need. Activity such as selection may bring further involvement, but in most cases there is little direct responsibility for expenditures.

Unit or department heads are more aware of the budget, their concept of it being largely determined by their share in the activities of the library. This tends to result in the question, how will the budget affect my department? Senior administrators frequently perceive such an attitude as selfish and may label it irresponsible—in contrast, of course, to the broad view of the administrator. This is a great simplification and leads to unnecessary argumentativeness. Any unit head is and must be concerned with the smooth functioning of the unit in the pursuit and achievement of its goals. That head will therefore regard the budget as a process and tend to ignore the disruptive discontinuities of fiscal years or possible conflicts arising from the goals and objectives of other units. At this level then the budget is best grasped as a series of interrelated programs and should be structured to show clearly the relationships between the various budget expenditures and the programs of the library.

The chief librarian, however, is concerned to synthesize the budgetary needs to each unit in order to quantify what must be asked for by grouping like expenditures. No matter what style of budget is used by the institution, whether it be an elaborate PPBS or a simple object expenditure approach, it is necessary at this stage to determine what gross quantities are being discussed—how many people, how many books, how many catalog cards—since these must be known before the costs of various program alternatives can be estimated.

A similar process is carried out at each successive stage, where the value of each budget proposal in relationship to the whole is reassessed while more and wider priorities are incorporated into the process of political judgement. The process is mitigated by the fact

Diagram 1. Budgetary Relationships within an Institution

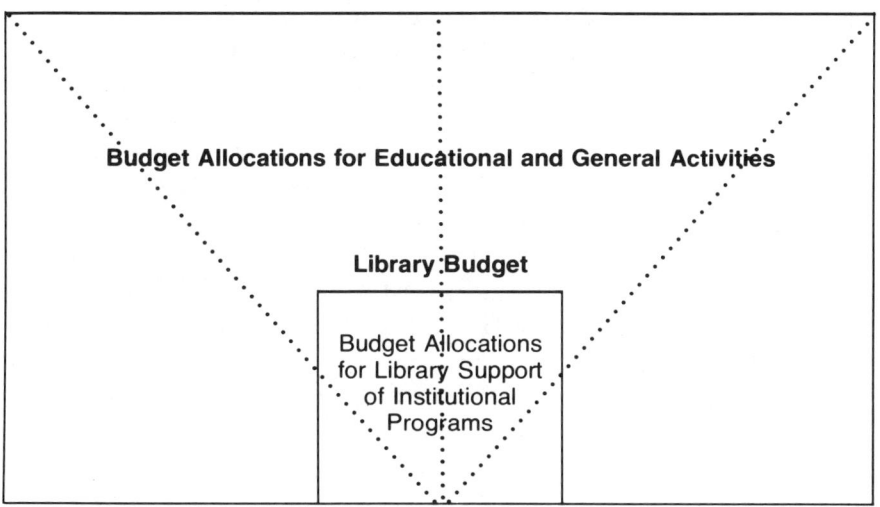

Cf. Standards for College Libraries, 8.1: "The amount of the library appropriation shall express a relationship to the total institutional budget for educational and general purposes." The relationship is both general and particular. As indicated in this diagram, the library relationship to each program will vary with the program.

that most of any budget proposal relates to mandated or otherwise unavoidable expenditure which implies that:

> Budgets are almost never actively reviewed as a whole in the sense of considering at once the value of all existing programs as compared to all possible alternatives. Instead this year's budget is based on last year's budget, with special attention given to a narrow range of increases or decreases.[4]

Nevertheless, any administrator may be called on to defend his budget request and must be prepared to justify the request, which in turn requires a thorough knowledge of the budget and an understanding of its programmatic implications.

To an accountant, business manager or auditor a budget is a set of accounts which control expenditures and prescribe methods for handling money to achieve certain ends. While this approach does not exclude flexibility, it is the business of such officers to ensure that flexibility is not used to avoid or abrogate the purposes for which the budget was set up. They will tend to regard the record of expenditure as a check on administrative responsibility.

A budget has therefore three aspects: planning, management and control.[5] All three are needed and all will be exercised in some degree by each staff member. Planning is closely associated with the action of budget preparation, but reflects the continuous process whereby the objectives of any organization are assessed, changed and restated. Management is the process by which the necessary resources are obtained and used in order to achieve the objectives of the institution. Control is the process by which adherence to policy is ensured. These aspects are complementary, though each may assume greater visibility at different periods during the fiscal year. The major planning effort, for example, usually precedes the beginning of the fiscal year, while the audit side of control will begin after its close. In consequence, those who are involved in one kind of activity rather than another will tend to be more visible when that activity is most important. This fact, though it may seem minor, plays an important part in governing intra-institutional relationships and must be kept in mind by any administrator.

Similarly, the budget itself assumes different forms. The request, which is usually presented in gross terms (such as total salaries, total book expenditures), is transformed in action into multitudes of individual transactions. In turn these are codified into sets of accounts that help reveal the relationship between the intent of the budget request and the activities of the year. All three phases are part of budgetary control. That control is exercised by many people in the course of making daily decisions. Such dispersal of activity is necessary, even though it introduces an element of confusion. The planning or budget officer must be concerned to ensure that this confusion does not become chaos. For example, an accounts clerk may have instructions to report when an individual book account is overdrawn and to stop processing invoices. A mechanism, however, must be provided for an overriding control since the greater goal of the library is to acquire books in response to need rather than in accordance with some artificial concept of distribution. The level at which each kind of control is exercised is therefore very important to the achievement of budgetary objectives.

Accident and chance play their part in any organization. Sudden, unexpected price increases are a fact of life, whether it be for a major piece of equipment or for a supply of card-stock. The fact of their occurrence is predictable, their incidence and effect is not. The budget itself and the system of control used must provide for such a situation. The chance to acquire a special book or collection may come but once and must be seized. Similar events may occur in almost any area. The goal of any control system should be to minimize the perturbation by channeling the effects properly. Rigidity of control tends to magnify the effects out of proportion. Flexibility, sensibly applied, will contain them without too much distortion of the original plan of expenditure.

Flexibility, response to change, or capitalization on some chance happening—all these indicate that budgeting is by no means a static activity, nor is the budget itself set once and for all without possiblity of alteration.

> Indeed, budget is a vehicle for the implementation of institutional plans and goals, rather than being, as in the past, simply a technique

for obtaining and dispensing the largest possible piece of the institutional or governmental financial pie.[6]

In summary then, a budget is a statement which identifiies in monetary terms the ways in which an institution will seek to achieve its goals during the period for which it is valid. It is not perceived similarly by all those who are affected by it and will require conversion into whatever mode is appropriate to each group, program or activity. It implies control and feedback to measure both conformity to the expressed or implicit goals and the degree of success attained in achieving those goals.

NOTES
1. Lyden and Miller (1965), p. 13.
2. Natchez and Bupp, p. 955.
3. Summers, p. 1175.
4. Davis, Dempster and Wildavsky, pp. 529–530.
5. Lyden and Miller (1965), pp. 27–29.
6. Galvin, (September 15, 1976), pp. 1834–1835.

Chapter 3

The Purpose of Budgetary Control

> *Control consists of comparing accomplishment against plans, and noting and correcting observed deviations. Its essence, then, is some sort of feedback. Scientific management demands control, for without it one cannot tell to what extent plans are being achieved. (Heinritz.)*

A budget is simply a planning document which sets out in summary form the categories and amounts of expenditures which appear necessary to maintain the library's programs. In the nature of things, it is impossible to predict with complete accuracy just what will occur during the year. The effects of price increases, whether for goods or services, are uneven. Some, which are externally imposed, such as rental for an accounting machine, must be paid, whatever the increase, unless it is decided to discontinue the existing activity and undertake the same work in some other manner. Such action may well be impossible because of other constraints. Equally, the effects of changes in consumer demand, as for example, an increase in circulation, may require the redirection of staff time. These and a multitude of similar examples that will occur to the reader indicate why any initial operating budget can only be approximation.

The closer a budget is to actuality, the easier it is to administer, and the more likely it is to allow the library to function smoothly. For this reason, it is very important (1) to enter the year with close estimates of likely activities and their costs and (2) to maintain close watch on how actual expenditures tally with those proposed at the beginning of the year.[1] Later chapters will examine prediction and monitoring in more detail. Here it is sufficient to summarize the kinds of information needed.

Library statistics are not usually comprehensive enough for true programming and budget forecasting.[2] Nor, for the most part, is it necessary to have all the detail suggested for true PPBS (Planning, Programming, Budgeting Systems) unless a major overhaul of the library's programs is contemplated. It is, however, essential to know the trends in various activities. If, for example, circulation is known to be increasing by about 8 percent each year, provision must be made for staff and supplies to cope with that increase. How this is done, is a political decision, but the statistics, if properly kept, will show that something must be done and will also indicate the size of the necessary action. The same reasoning applies to all other activities internal to the library.

Information on external influences must also be fed into the budget process. Price increases for goods and services may be announced publicly (a good example of this is increases in postal rates); or they may become available only on receipt of an invoice or a letter from an individual supplier (maintenance cost increases are usually made known in this manner); or they may be made available after the fact as is the case with the various analyses of price indexes published in the literature. Not all of these are solely library-related. Fuel costs, for example, affect the whole institution, but their secondary effects may include reductions in the amount available for other kinds of expenditure.

A moment's contemplation of all changes which may affect the budget suggests that the library administrator must take on the role of Argus. No one person could, however, maintain such vigilance. The administrator must therefore rely on others for much of this information. Most institutions maintain a central office with responsiblity for budget and planning, although this responsibility may be assigned to someone with other duties as well. It is vital for the health of the library to maintain good relations with the people responsible for the fiscal administration of the institution.[3] There is a tendency among academics to disregard such mundane matters as "accounting" though at the same time they complain if their needs are not met. There is nothing ignoble about money, nor about knowing how to use it properly.[4] Everything that is done in an academic institution is paid for. If it is paid for by running into debt, sooner or later that debt must also be paid. If it is sizeable, the results may be bankruptcy, which has happened disturbingly often recently, or drastic cuts in programs, at which those who caused the overdraft are the most likely to express bewilderment. Sound fiscal policy is therefore a guarantee of the health of the institution and of the library.

Institutions are subject to the controls imposed by those who provide the money. The hope is that they will understand the goals of the institution and set up controls which help to achieve those goals. Such controls carry with them the need for the institution itself to set up policies and procedures for the apportionment and control of the budget. It is necessary for the library administrator to know these policies and procedures and to be able to apply them to the library. Exceptions will frequently be needed, and it is more satisfactory to all if requests for such exceptions can be discussed within a common framework. Once again, such a process is smoothed by the establishment of good working relations at all levels, whether with a vice-president or with the head of accounting. As an example, libraries need to be sure that renewal payments for subscriptions are processed promptly. If new procedures such as cyclical payments set up by the accounting office interfere with this smooth flow, it may be necessary to request that all invoices or vouchers from the library receive first priority. Such a request made out of the blue could well meet resistance, and even if it were imposed by administrative fiat might be subverted by a resentful staff. The same request made in a context of mutual understanding could result in a modified procedure that enables both units to achieve their goals.

Even more important is a feeling for the ambience of the institution. There is frequently a great difference between public stance and private action. This does not imply dishonesty or conniving—simply that public debate over budgets or plans tend to be conducted in simplistic terms, while those who must maintain daily activities have to make the best possible guess at the likely outcome and plan accordingly, since it is not possible to suspend operations pending resolution of differences at the public level, Such situations require that the library administrator have a sense of the flexibility available to the institution in order to avoid making a commitment that cannot be honored because of changed circumstances.

On a more basic level, such matters as the rigidity of the budget structure and the rules concerning the reallocation of savings, must be known by the library administrator. Some funding agencies—for example, state legislatures—may set limits on the amount of transferability between budget categories. Some, indeed, present line budgets and allow no flexibility, but most recognize that many factors are unpredictable and allow a degree of over or under expenditure providing that the general goals are met. Most librarians are familiar with the sudden pot of gold made available late in the year for the purchase of books. Most, too, are aware of the strains this causes within the fabric of the library. It is, however, a continuing possibility, since it is exceedingly unlikely that any institutional budget will ever be spent exactly as it was set up at the beginning of the fiscal year. Appointments that do not take place, unexpected resignations and similar happenings guarantee that there will be unspent money available at some time during the year. If these savings can be transferred to other units, a transfer will be made. The better organized institutions plan for this eventuality in order to make the best use of such savings.[5] Libraries, as a "bottomless pit," can always use extra money.[6] The key to its successful use is to be ready, and to have prepared the appropriate administrators so that the transfer can be made at the best time and in the best manner. If it is possible, and it *is* when the librarian can convince the right people, the extra amount that can be allowed, say for books, can be estimated in advance and added early in the year, thus permitting smooth planning for purchasing and avoiding an end of the year rush. This is only one example of the way in which good relations can bring about a sympathetic understanding of the library and its needs, and why such relations are important for the librarian who has responsibility for the budget.

The difference between decisions on policy and decisions on money is frequently misunderstood. In general the budget reflects policy decisions by attempting to ensure that the amounts and the distribution of the available money will match the needs of the various programs which result from decisions on policy. It is true that, occasionally, money or, rather, the lack of it, will be a determinant in whether a particular program can be undertaken. Further, in a time of financial stress, it may be necessary to reduce expenditures and on such an occasion the details of the budget will assist in making decisions.

Policy decisions are those that determine what services will be given, what resources will be acquired and what changes will be made. They result from a careful consideration of all the relevant facts, including financial ones. Once made, if the decision is to be implemented, provision must be made for its cost. This does not always mean new money, but may also include transfers from one program or one category of expenditure to another. The latter kinds of adjustments are not always taken into account when decisions are made. Such an omission may well result in failure of the new program or in a series of ad hoc adjustments which damage other programs. It is highly desirable to require, before making major policy decisions, that a forward estimate of costs be prepared for, say, a five-year period. Such a projection will reveal where and when monetary support is needed and whether all factors have been taken into account. That is to say, policy decisions must be fiscally responsible, but, except in unusual circumstances, financial matters are not the only factor to be considered when making a decision on policy.

All such decision-making must, however, be carried out within the institutional framework. The standard procedure has been to prepare budget proposals in advance of any fiscal year for presentation to and consideration by the institutional administrators responsible for making budgetary decisions. The difficulties encountered by most institutions in maintaining their programs when faced by mounting costs and decreasing revenues has introduced a completely new budgetary process, which is frequently described, somewhat euphemistically, as the reallocation of resources. Generally this means a reassessment of all programs and their costs and may be a substitute for the normal budgeting process or may be superimposed upon it. Instead of preparing an asking budget, the library administrator may be called upon to prepare a budget request based upon the reallocation or redistribution of existing funds, or some portion thereof. Preparing such a budget is quite different from preparing one which adds new money, whether for inflation or for new needs. It requires a reexamination of goals, of existing commitments and of possibilities under the new guidelines. The question of priorities becomes of critical importance, particularly since so many library operations are interdependent. With a steady budget, a reduced one, or even an increasing one which cannot cover the effects of inflation, it is clear that a library cannot continue as before. It therefore becomes a question of determining what must still be done, what that will cost and, in a sense, what will be left over for everything else. The success of such an operation will depend not only on the wisdom with which choices are made, but on the accuracy of past records from which future projections must be made.

In such a situation the allocation of the budget clearly takes on political overtones, and it is essential that the administrator be able to separate fact from emotional reaction. Some expectations will have to be deferred, some programs modified, either at once or during the course of the fiscal year; but, if the right decisions have been made, the general goals of the library will be maintained.

The making of these choices is, no doubt, an unwelcome added burden; but, if the library staff concerned is financially ingenious, much can be done in the course of the year to redirect and manipulate funds to sustain the decisions made and to lessen their side effects. This is a large part of the meaning of budgetary control, which, as well as having a role in ensuring fiscal responsibility, is concerned with the directing of funds toward the achievement of the library's goals.

The existence of the restraints briefly sketched above requires that budgets be watched much more closely than was the case in years of high funding. Because the working margins are so small, it is essential to know where strains are likely to appear and the signs of their appearance. If budgetary control is too decentralized, the likelihood that such strains will not be detected early enough is increased. For example, it has usually been the practice not to exercise any restraint on the growth of the serials allocation. When there always seemed to be enough money for other purchases, and extra money was made available each year to meet inflation, uncontrolled growth could be accommodated. Now, however, it is more than likely for any library that the increased cost of serial subscriptions must be balanced by decreases in other expenditures on materials. If no attempt is made to monitor such expenditures, the warning signs may not be heeded until balance can only be restored by massive cancellations.

Another example of the care that must be taken is the control of supplies, which happen generally to be common to most operations. If no attempt is made to record and to estimate the use made of these supplies by various departments, the library may suddenly find that there is not enough money left to replenish supplies of a critical item such as circulation cards. In such a case, one of the library's basic goals could only be met by taking money from some other items since it is inconceivable that a library could cease to issue materials.

These considerations may seem a fragile base on which to rest a case for centralized control, but the examples could be multiplied many times. The word "control" itself is often misunderstood, and taken to mean only regulation, domination or restraint. Some of these elements may indeed have to be present, but its true aim is to coordinate, balance and monitor the successful fulfillment of the basic plan.

Because orders and requests for payment are derived from a very wide range of sources, they must, for ease of handling, be channeled through one operation, usually an accounting department. If this is done, then that department is better able to maintain records of expenditure which can be compared with proposed expenditures and the resulting analysis used to redirect the library's activities, if that is necessary. All librarians are familiar with the situation where no one quite knows all that is happening because the responsibility for reporting is too fragmented to make that reporting meaningful without laborious reconstruction, usually after the fact. This simply cannot be allowed to happen with financial reporting, since after-the-fact adjustment is, in the nature of things, impossible. Balance for such centralization is necessary and is provided by widespread consultation, particularly when budgets are prepared. Information on the progress of various expenditures must also be available to all responsible for those expenditures, so that they are able to discuss intelligently alternative needs and patterns of action designed to meet those needs. Such a consultative mechanism will help in maintaining confidence among the library staff, even, or perhaps especially, when unpalatable alternatives must be chosen. Finally, an informed staff is better able to represent the library to outside parties, whether students, faculty or other administrators.

Accountability is a word frequently found in management literature. Within most academic institutions the director, dean or head librarian is held by the administration to be accountable to that administration for the successful running of the library. In this, that official has no choice. Tasks may be delegated, even the responsibility for whole areas of activity, but the ultimate responsibility cannot be shared in this manner. For that reason the head librarian must retain a very close interest in the budgetary process, even while the actual control of daily activity may be in the hands of others. Advice, consultation and all other methods of involvement should be sought and will strengthen the head librarian's hand in negotiating with the administration, but none of these is an adequate substitute for intimate, personal knowledge.

NOTES

1. Heinritz, p. 21.
2. David Palmer, reported by Harold Jenkins, cites the kinds of statistics needed and the rationale behind keeping statistics.
3. The importance of such relationships is stressed by Summers when he describes the professionalization of budgeting, contrasting the past, when the

library administrator was the sole expert, with the present, when budgets at all stages are reviewed by knowledgeable analysts and budget experts. The argument is applied to legislative bodies, but it is equally applicable to the large academic institution.

4. Robins (1973), pp. 5–6.

5. Dix (1972, pp. 8–18) provides an amusing and stimulating discussion on the needs and relationships of a library within an institution in a time of fiscal crisis.

6. Munn, p. 52.

Chapter 4

Preliminary Budget Analysis

> *The current operating budget is a one-year segment of the program plan.* (Robins, 1973.)

While this chapter is intended primarily to deal with the analysis of the library budget in relation to the annual budget request, it is necessary to remember that the library, perhaps more than any other academic unit, operates in a continuum. It is no more possible to prepare a budget request in a vacuum, than it is to shelve periodical issues in order of receipt, regardless of title, for open access. Each activity must have regard to past experience and future need, the budget particularly so. Periodical issues can be reshelved; dollars cannot be respent.

Library budgets reflect the budgetary style of the parent institution. It may be helpful, therefore, to summarize briefly the basic kinds of budgetary systems in use by academic institutions. Five such types may be identified, although there will also be subtypes of each. These are:

1) The object classification budget, which has been the traditional approach and which is based primarily on kinds of expenditure.

2) The program budget, which is based largely on the measurement of programs with consequently less emphasis on the objects purchased, and their relationship to organizational units.

3) The performance budget, which is based primarily on the establishment of relationship between the investment of resources and the production of services.

4) The Planning, Programming, Budget System, which combines both the preceding methods, adding cost-analysis and management by objective.

5) The formula budget, which is based on the use of standards and quantitative modes in the allocation of funds.[1]

It clearly would require too extensive a treatment to consider each of these alternatives in every case, and the assumption will therefore be made that some kind of performance or program budget is the most common method. In fact most institutions will follow a mixed budgetary model, a common one being a budget summarized in line items, but which requires performance or program data in the justification and bases the line summary on that data.[2] Moreover, the form a budget takes will vary with the needs and purposes of whoever is handling it.

At some time during the year (or once in two years if the institution follows the biennial plan of financing), the institution will require the responsible officials to prepare a budget request. Depending on the place of the library within the hierarchy, the library's budget requests may be submitted independently or as part of a group of allied services. The former is the more usual and allows better for the presentation of the library's requests.

The timing of this request will vary with the institution, but the general pattern is for it to be well in advance of the fiscal year concerned. This allows adequate time for consideration within the institution before the final request is presented to the controlling body, such as the state legislature. In fact, the time for budget preparation is now frequently so far advanced that those who must prepare it often cannot estimate accurately the degree of success or failure of budget plans for the current year and must extrapolate from the previous year instead. Such a situation naturally complicates planning and usually means that the budgets arrived at in this manner can be conceived only in gross terms. Nevertheless, even to arrive at such generalized statements, a great amount of detail is required. Those who suffer through such preparatory work frequently wonder at its utility, since the guidelines may change drastically before the actual budget is fixed and allocated. The preparation does, however, require the analysis of needs and expectations and provides a better framework within which to allocate what is eventually received.

The guidelines or instructions that accompany requests for budget submissions vary as widely as the time. They may set no limits but simply ask the administrator to set out program needs. A percentage (or a dollar figure) limit may be set on expansion, and this may in turn be different for personnel costs and material costs. An inflation allowance may be provided for purchases, whether or not any increase in the purchasing program is considered. Conversely, a reduction may be requested in total expenditure, with or without guidelines for the different portions of the budget. Frequently, a preferential ordering of requests is asked for.

In responding to such requests, the library administrator is usually in a very different position from the average academic administrator. A department or college is principally concerned with teaching and therefore has a budget which is almost entirely composed of personnel costs. These costs can be related to enrollment projections; and, while there may be unhappiness over inability to expand a teaching program, in general the intention is to provide enough teachers to teach the courses to be offered. By contrast, a library is concerned with a very wide range of services, whose volume it is unable to control (perhaps even to predict) and with a very substantial purchasing program for materials. The interactions of the several portions of a library budget are complex and sometimes unpredictable, requiring a greater degree of flexibility than most other administrative areas. Relationships between student enrollment and library use cannot be reduced to a formula.[3] More students probably mean more library use, but it will be distributed unevenly among the various units of the library. The acquisition of materials is affected more by program changes than by enrollment. In particular, a drop in enrollment does not mean that fewer materials can be bought, unless in discrete areas such as reserves. The effects of inflation play a large role in determining the volume of acquisitions, and fluctuations in this kind of program cannot easily be matched by fluctuations in processing costs, which are principally for personnel. In such cases it is necessary to recognize that at some times there will be excess labor available or to accept a state where there is an almost permanent backlog of some kind. The choice made will depend on the condition which corresponds most closely to the goals of the library.

It is, however, inherent in the nature of most library activities that they can be modified only slowly and with great attention to side effects. This inertia is most easily demonstrated in the areas of technical operations where the ordering and receipt of material is followed at intervals of time by cataloging, processing and shelving. The process, however it may be varied, cannot arbitrarily be halted without defeating its entire purpose. It is also a process which may extend over a considerable period of time so that the effects of this year's orders may not show up in shelving needs for perhaps another year or even longer, especially if extra activities such as binding must be undertaken. Thus, even a large diminution in funds for purchasing materials may not in turn affect cataloging and processing activities for a further budget year, by which time special funds may have been made available. Such inertial effects are not confined to technical services; but are elsewhere more subtle, evidenced by the slowness with which library users will adopt new services or recognize that old ones are no longer available. The author will remember forever the professor who received a request to revise his reserve reading list and came to the library to protest that he knew what was good for his students and his list was the best they could have, his only problem being that the reserve-book room had been moved three years before and he could not find it. More concretely, the long delivery schedules for equipment or repairs may delay moves which are intended to relieve congestion or to enable new services to be given more effectively; and in the meantime books are piling up or work habits are generated which will have to be unlearned. All such factors must be taken into account when planning a budget, and must be explained to those responsible for its review since, alas, most nonlibrarians take a very simplistic view of a library's operations.

For the purposes of this study it will be assumed that a normal sequence of events can be expected: preparation of a budget estimate for next year about halfway through the current year, consideration of this request over a period of about two months, its incorporation into the institutional request, and the preparation of an operating budget shortly before the new year commences. Any number of variations is possible, and these will be considered when appropriate.

ANALYSIS OF THE BUDGET REQUEST DOCUMENT

The request for budget submissions is prepared by the central administration and is based on reasonable expectations for the year ahead (or the biennium if such is the institutional requirement). The request usually consists of three parts:
   (1) policy instructions;
   (2) procedural instructions;
   (3) financial statements.

The policy instructions set out the guidelines to be used in preparing the budgetary requests and state limits on expansion, or requirements for reduction. These may provide for adding or subtracting personnel in relationship to programs whether by formula or according to priorities. An amount or a percentage may be provided for inflation, or requests may have to include such a factor. Provision may be made for new programs and will usually include instructions relating to the necessary justification. Limitations may be placed on the degree of change that can be made within any budgetary element (as, for example, transfers between personnel and material expenses) or special justification may be required for changes greater than an arbitrary percentage. The amount of detail will depend on how finely the budget is required to be broken down.

Each part of this explanation must be studied carefully for its effect on the budget request, particularly in relation to the documentation required and the interrelationship between elements. If, for example, the statement is made that no new positions may be requested, a request for money to buy more materials would be impossible, unless internal adjustments could be made to shift personnel resources into processing, even though the instructions allow such a request to be made. The guidelines will also set out the institutional priorities and these must be studied in relation to the library's own needs and priorities. Here, for example, the institution may give priority to increased teaching work load, based on enrollment or credit hour projections. While the library does not generate credit hours, it is reasonable to expect that increased enrollment will be reflected in greater library use; and this must be pointed out, even if the instructions do not allow for such changes in academic support units.

Finally, it is important to understand how goals, priorities and program proposals are to be set out and related to budget requests. This may require that the entire budget be constructed, or reconstructed on a program basis or simply that requests for added funds must be so treated. Whichever is the case, it is necessary to analyse the library's expenditures in order to relate them to a programmatic statement.

The procedural requirements are usually fairly straightforward and consist mostly of instructions relating to the budget timetable or where to put what information. When computers handle the collation and checking of budget requests, the details may become very cumbersome. It is difficult for the unmechanized layman to understand the need for some instructions; but woebetide the unwary person who uses the wrong format, setting out numbers in the normal fashion as $2,173,158 instead of the required $2 173 158. Although it may seem unimportant, adhering to such instructions helps to create or strengthen the sense of trust which wise administrators cultivate with the budget office staff.

The most usual format for setting out financial information is to use columns summarizing the various areas or lines of expenditure, showing the current year, the year for which a budget request is to be made and perhaps the succeeding year. The number of lines will depend on the detail required in the breakdown. The most usual subdivisions are "personnel-related expenses" and "allotment" or some similar term for payment for things. For libraries a separate subdivision may be made for library materials or for binding. Occasionally library materials and equipment are regarded as capital expenditure. That is unusual, although in a cost-accounting sense it is true, since books are in most cases bought with permanent retention in mind. The finer the subdivisions are made, the more work the budget requires and the less flexibility is usually available.

After the budget request has been received and analyzed, the next requirement is to check out the accuracy of the base budget recorded in the request. This is required not so much to test the figures, although the best budget offices may err if the information is complex, but to recheck the relationship of the printed budget to the operating budget. As will be discussed later, during any one year many temporary or permanent budget adjustments may be made. These may obscure the actual permanent budget available, and it is necessary to reassess that budget before proceeding to further modifications. It may, for example, be desirable to make permanent an adjustment that was formerly temporary, and this should be a first concern in preparing any budget. Also, the printed budget will reflect the original plan for the year and contains money represented by vacant positions or money for expected purchases of goods or services that were not made. An initial estimate of funds available from these sources will help determine the degree of flexibility available before asking for new funds. In this connection, however, it is important to be aware of the institution's rules on the handling of vacant positions. Transfer between classes (*e.g.*, from academic to clerical) may be forbidden or subject to special rules. If the institution operates on an accrual basis, unexpended funds, which have been encumbered, may be permitted to carry over. If not, then the encumbrances will be a first charge against the next year. Even so, it is possible to prepare some initial guide to the availability of funds for new uses within the existing budget, and that is the principal objective of examining the budget as printed.

ANALYSIS OF THE EXISTING LIBRARY BUDGET

Once this initial analysis has been completed, the next step is to analyze the entire library budget.[4] Naturally, it would be impossible to do this from scratch after receipt of the budget request; so it is recommended that the library administration maintain an ongoing examination, which can be updated relatively simply. It is, however, important to wait for the request to be received before completing this step because the instructions may materially affect the degree and kind of analysis required.

Most budgets have two divisions, one for personnel-related expenses and the other for goods and services purchased. Because libraries purchase a great quantity of one particular thing, namely "books," there may be a separate division for books. The names for these budgetary divisions are as varied as the institutions responsible. For consistency's sake, the terms "personnel-related expenses" and "goods and services" will be used for the two major kinds of expenditure, and the term "library materials" will be used to cover books, periodicals, binding and other similar purchases.

Whatever terms are used, it is useful to remember that the budget describes intended purchases of two commodities—time and things. Time is represented principally by people employed, full- and part-time, but also by various contracts for services such as maintenance of equipment or computer services. The amount of time purchased depends on the cost per hour of that time, and the money available to pay for it. Things are represented by a much greater number of items and include supplies as mundane as pencils and paper, ranging up to major purchases of equipment. Some items will therefore be counted in large quantities—for example, one million circulation cards. Others will be purchased singly—for example, catalog card cabinets. The variety of things purchased each year will depend on the needs of that year, although basic needs such as supplies will tend to be a constant factor. But, whatever difference may exist between one budget and another, each will consist of amounts set aside for the purchase of time and things, and this concept is a sound guide in a budget analysis.

The purpose of a budget analysis is to see whether the intended distribution of expenditures is matched by actual expenditures, and what the differences, if any, are. Most budget statements contain a cover sheet which sets out broad categories, followed by detail sheets, most of which are given over to a listing of personnel.

For ease of comparison in presenting sample figures or budgetary proposals, all such figures given in this discussion are based on an imaginary library, with reference when necessary to other libraries or to similar kinds of budgets. This library, created for the exercise of the imaginative talents of both author and reader, is that of a moderately large academic library, possessed of most features common to such libraries—branches, several departments and the usual budgetary problems. (See Appendix.) For such a library the general budget statement may appear as shown in Table 1.

Table 1. The Budget of the State University Libraries
The State University
University Libraries
Budget Number 550/50
Budget Code 1000

Personal Related Expenses			
Full-time positions*		$1,755,000	
Wages		235,000	
	Subtotal	$1,990,000	$1,990,000
Allotment			
Goods and services		$200,000	$200,000
Library materials		950,000	950,000
Reserve		$60,000	$60,000
Total Expenditures			$3,200,000
	Total Income	$45,000	

* 172 positions listed separately in an attachment.

PERSONNEL-RELATED EXPENSES

The detail provided will vary with the institution, but it is customary to separate the various classes of employees. The names used for each class are by no means consistent, but, by and large, the following classes of employee will be represented:

(a) *Professional.* These positions may be academic, faculty or nonacademic professional. A separate listing may be shown for administrators. If the positions are academic, listings may be by rank. It may be arranged by department, but this is unusual.

The listing will also indicate the source of the salary, which is important in the case of joint appointments or positions funded from endowments or similar funds.

(b) *Staff.* These positions may include nonacademic professionals, but more usually will be paraprofessionals and any category of employee within the nonexempt classification of the Department of Labor.

(c) *Clerical.* These positions generally include all classified positions other than those included under "Staff." Frequently such a grouping is defined by a union contract. Possibly it may be further subdivided to cover nonclerical employees, such as janitors or drivers, in which case more than one union contract may be involved.

Note: There is an increasing tendency of these groupings to be defined externally, whether by union, state, or Federal contracts or regulations.

(d) *Part-time Employees.* These positions are more permanent than those paid from wage budgets, but may require annual renegotiation and may not have available the same fringe benefits as permanent, full-time positions. In some institutions where strong central control is exercised over all full-time positions, these part-time appointments may represent the only flexibility available. A further class of part-time appointment sometimes available is the graduate assistantship. In most libraries, however, this is not an important source of personnel.

(e) *Wages.* This portion of the budget is intended to cover all hourly employment, both student and nonstudent. In some institutions only students may be hired on hourly wages and all other employees must be full- or part-time regular employees. Such a stipulation severely restricts a library and is an undesirable restraint. Each institution will also have rules concerning such terms of employment as maximum weekly hours and rates of pay, though in general these are based on federal regulations.

The most important action in analyzing personnel-related expenses is to allocate them to the various library programs. A true program analysis requires that each position be divided according to activity, since this is the only way to discover the exact cost of each activity within the library.[5] Such care is not usually necessary; equally useful results can be achieved by the allocation of the gross costs represented by whole positions. The inexactness of this method is balanced by knowledge of the activities being carried on in each department. Moreover, unless one is, for example, making a cost-benefit analysis of an automated circulation system, there is no great advantage to knowing exactly how much time is spent on circulation-related activities in a branch Library, since these activities will have to be carried on in that location and only dramatic changes in work load are likely to affect the cost. Information of that kind should be provided by the appropriate staff member.

The analysis will indicate full- and part-time positions and wages in each administrative area and should indicate also exisiting vacancies. Table 2 shows a sample distribution which will be used as a basis for discussion.

This distribution indicates the personnel-related cost to the library of its major units of activity. The information should be shared with all library administrators, including unit heads; although in cases where the institution requires that personal salaries be confidential, any figures that reveal individual salaries should be omitted in statements released widely. Information of this kind assists unit heads in budget-planning, because it enables them to see their own units in a general context. Without such a background it is difficult, if not impossible, to develop proposals for change.

Of course, it is important to know what is done by the people represented by these amounts of money, and to know what other costs, such as materials or supplies, are associated with their activity. At this stage, however, the analysis is concerned with gross distributions. Administrative costs, for example, which include the directors and their staff, accounting and personnel, account for $184,000, representing an overhead of about 10 percent (9 percent of the total expenditure). Technical services account for approximately 39 percent, branch libraries for 10 percent and the remaining central library costs for 42 percent. Whether this distribution is in line with the goals and needs of the library can only be determined by the examination of other factors, but it is necessary to know the existing distribution in order to establish the desirability of change.

One further fact which must be determined at this time is the number and the location of vacancies. It is important also to determined whether the vacancy has caused problems; and, if so, problems of what kind. If not, the position may well be a suitable candidate for transfer to another activity. Many vacancies, however, are of a transitory nature. For example, the turnover rate in the cataloging typing pool may be 30 percent a year. In such circumstances, it would actually be surprising not to have a vacancy at the time of budget examination, but such a vacancy would be of no significance, at least in budget terms, since it would usually be the intention to fill it as soon as possible. Where, however, a longstanding vacancy results either from difficulty in finding a suitable replacement or from uncertainty over the need for the activity involved, such a vacancy should be considered for transfer, or perhaps for collapsing. The budget or planning Officer should, metaphorically and perhaps literally, red circle such positions for further consideration during the process of budget formulation.

Because this budget review is being carried out during the course of a fiscal year, the actual expenditures should also be examined to see whether they are in line with the original budget. In most categories of personnel-related expenditure this will equate with whatever temporal portion of the year has passed. Certain variations are possible, depending, for example, on the manner in which annual raises are provided for clerical positions and whether other

Table 2. Personnel-Related Expenses—Departmental* Distribution.

Department	Professional		Semi-Professional		Clerical		Wages	Total
	No.	Cost	No.	Cost	No.	Cost	Cost	Cost
Administration	5	$98,000	2	$22,000	8	$54,000	$10,000	$184,000
Acquisitions	4	58,000	3	30,000	8	59,000	15,000	162,000
Cataloging	12	181,000	4	42,000	20	157,000	20,000	400,000
Serials	3	48,000	3	27,000	15	110,000	25,000	210,000
General Services	5	76,000	3	26,000	8	62,000	30,000	194,000
Lending Services	2	34,000	3	30,000	14	95,000	40,000	199,000
Reference Services	10	157,000	3	26,000	8	56,000	30,000	269,000
Reserve Services	2	30,000	1	9,000	5	35,000	25,000	99,000
Special Collections	2	38,000	1	10,000	2	17,000	10,000	75,000
Science	2	32,000	1	9,000	3	24,000	10,000	51,000
Engineering	1	16,000	1	10,000	2	15,000	10,000	51,000
Life Sciences	2	32,000	1	9,000	3	21,000	10,000	72,000
	50	$800,000	26	$250,000	96	$705,000	$235,000	$1,990,000

*Departmental definitions are provided in Appendix One.

raises are provided concurrent with a new budget year or on anniversary dates. Corrections of this kind should be made at this time. In addition, it is possible that a replacement has been hired at a lower or a higher salary. The most likely area of variation is, however, in wage budget expenditure, since this may be affected by use of work-study students (payments for whom do not show up in the library budget) or by the diversion of temporary funds to cover a problem situation. Since it is almost impossible to predict accurately wage expenditure by unit, some will be ahead and some behind the proportionate amount of thier allocation. Such variations should also be noted for exploration. In this way a matrix can be developed showing planned, actual and predicted expenditures, both by class of employee and by unit of employment. A sample matrix is shown in Diagram 2. Wage expenditure for the whole library over the fiscal year is converted in this diagram into a precentile. If all expenditures were incurred evenly throughout the year, cumulative expenditure would be represented by the diagonal line (e). Although such a distribution is unlikely ever to be the case, mainly because academic institutions do not operate on a uniform basis throughout the year, it forms a useful base against which to compare actual or projected expenditures. Moreover, unless the budget is to be overspent, all other lines should converge with this line toward the upper right-hand corner of the diagram. Line (a) represents actual expenditure for the period of the fiscal year to date. Line (a^1) represents a projection of this expenditure pattern to the end of the year and line (a^2) represents the initial planned or expected pattern of expenditure. Inspection of the diagram will indicate that both planned and actual expenditure reflect a decrease in cumulative rate in September, when work-study students are made available; while both the planned and projected expenditures expect an increase in the cumulative rate of expenditure in January, when new federal base rates will come into effect. Comparison of the lines will also reveal substantial over-expenditure which, if continued, would lead to an actual budget deficit. While it is presumed that steps would be taken to correct such a situation, either by reducing expenditure or by adding money to the wage budget, the purpose of this analysis would be to

38 / *Budgetary Control in Academic Libraries*

Diagram 2. Analysis and Projection of Total Wage Expenditures.

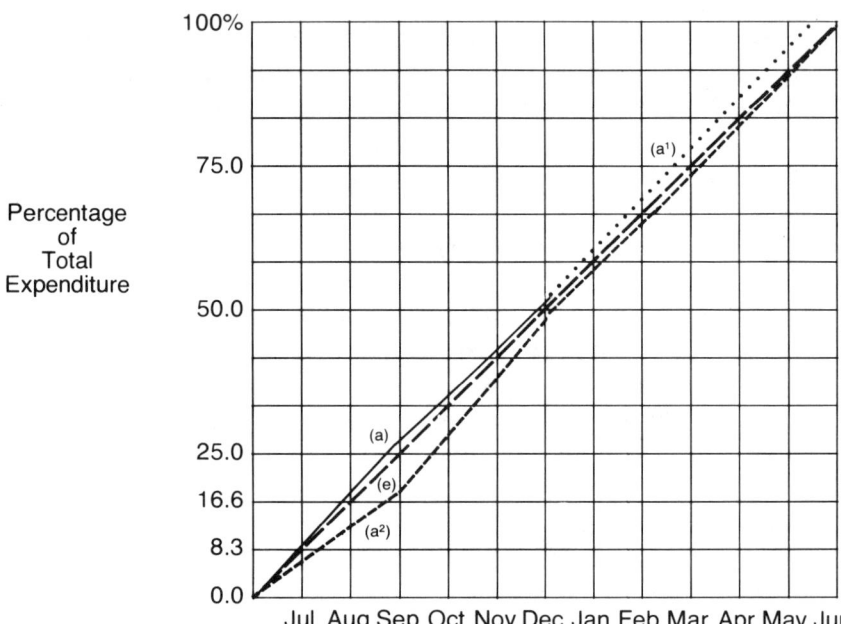

——(a)——	Actual Total Expenditure to Date (July–December).
....(a¹)....	Projected Expenditure for Year Based on Actual Expenditures.
——(a²)——	Planned or Expected Expenditure.
——(e)——	Theoretical Even Distribution.

determine the cause of the deviation from the original forecast of expenditure. If the cause is an increase in work load, or special factors such as unexpected new program requirements, it will be necessary to incorporate into future budget plans sufficient support for the activity, whether by more wages, by new full-time positions or by substitutional transfer of expenditures. It may, on the other hand, represent the library's response to unexpected long-term vacancies, or a special project which had to be completed in a short time. In such instances the overexpenditure will correct itself. All investigations would, of course, seek to relate the deviation in expenditure to programs or units in order to ascertain what specific response is required.

GOODS AND SERVICES

In the sample budget statement, $200,000 is allowed for total expenditure within this category. Many institutions divide this category into subcategories on the budget statement itself. If this is the case, it may be necessary to obtain approval of any variations. Such line control can be extremely vexatious, since the majority of exception requests would be for small amounts. But the more important effect is the complete loss of flexibility, which makes it impossible to respond quickly either to emergencies or to a necessary shift of priorities. In addition, it may be required either to obtain external approval for all purchases over a stated amount, or even to forward all purchase requests to some agency for approval and processing. This is more common in systems than in single institutions and particularly so for those under the control of a department of government.

It is assumed here that responsibility for allocation and control is internal to the library. Even where this is not the case, the analysis of expenditures is a fundamental part of budget preparation.

Most institutions have standardized classes of expenditure, for which the nomenclature may differ, and these classes are generally coded to enable the institutions to derive total expenditure figures. Occasionally the coding may be inappropriate for a library (*e.g.,* "instructional supplies" meaning paper, etc., for use in a classroom), but it is generally possible to come to an accommodation.

In this case the distribution is assumed to be as shown in Table. 3.

It is not a common practice to charge heat, light, janitorial services and the like to each administrative unit, although records of such expenditures may be kept centrally. Raffel and Shisko demonstrate the important of these and other indirect costs when carrying out a cost-benefit analysis,[6] and for true program budget-planning accurate knowledge of such costs is essential. For the most part, however, librarians do not have to concern themselves with overhead costs of this kind. An exception may arise if or when an institution is faced with a planned reduction in fuel costs or if a true cost is needed for the recovery of a prorated portion from a customer seeking shared cataloging, computer services or contractual reference services.

Most of these expenditures are "fixed" by the library's programs. It is possible, but not essential, to prorate all expenditures to units within the library. An example of this approach is sketched by Rogers and Weber.[7] Such a detailed assignment of costs would be necessary in a library where each unit had a high level of autonomy, or in support of a program budget. In general the amount of expenditure for such general purposes is but a small proportion of

Table 3. Goods and Services.

Object Class	Type of Expenditure	Amount
200	Supplies	40,000
300	Communications	20,000
310	Maintenance	20,000
340	Repairs and Renovations	15,000
370	Rentals	25,000
400	Computer Services	30,000
500	Miscellaneous	10,000
600	Travel and Research Support	15,000
700	Equipment	25,000
	TOTAL	$200,000

the cost of each unit. Exceptions are, of course, the supplies needed by cataloging to produce cards, or by circulation if cards are used, and the maintenance costs for microform readers, photocopiers, etc. It is, however, both possible and necessary to keep records of items purchased in bulk, or subject to annual contracts.

Within the budget outlined above, it is likely that at least $150,000 will be spent on basic needs. Supplies consist almost entirely of items required in daily activity. Communication costs can be reduced only by reducing the number of telephones or the number of letters sent out. The first may be possible, though its accomplishment is a strong indication that the original expenditure was unjustified. The second reduction is highly unlikely, since libraries are in the business of communication. Other expenditures within this category are TWX or TELEX costs, telefacsimile transmission costs, perhaps a delivery contract with an agency such as United Parcels Service. Maintenance agreements covering machinery in use in the library are essential. Major repairs and renovations may be postponed but, in general, doors, lights, chairs and so on must be repaired if the library is to remain functional.

Rental equipment is a major feature of modern libraries, particularly in areas subject to rapid technological change. Moreover, rental or leasing arrangements may be the only way to obtain such equipment within the limits of the operating budget. Such expenditures relate directly to program priorities and will change only if the programs themselves are changed. The choice between renting and purchasing equipment relates both to the possiblity of obsolescence and to budgetary constraints. In an area such as computer technology, the rate of change in the hardware is very rapid. This change is not merely in style or model, but relates to the fundamental purpose of the equipment. Increases both in storage capacity and in speed of retrieval mean that even though the cost of a later-generation model will be greater, the unit cost will decrease. Baumol and Marcus[8] present an eloquent discussion of this factor as basic to long-term planning. For such reasons, it is frequently more economic for a library to rent or lease rather than to purchase machinery which may shortly be superseded, since in this way advantage may be taken of improvements, which would otherwise be available only at the cost of entire replacement or expensive modification. Care must, of course, be taken to ensure that the contract does, in fact, provide for updating. Computers are not the only kind of equipment where rental may be considered. The same arguments apply to photocopying machinery. It is, for example, desirable to avoid a situation where a sudden increase in need forces the library to buy or rent extra copiers, or a decrease (*e.g.*, as a result of taking OCLC catalog cards) leaves the library with an expensive, unused high-speed copier.

Not all budgets include funds for equipment, since this may be regarded as a capital expenditure. Nevertheless, most libraries purchase some equipment each year, and certain kinds of expenditures are predicted by ongoing library activity. An example of such predicated expenditure is the need for catalog cabinets. If cards are being produced, they have to be stored, and at a certain stage, usually predictable within rough time-limits, catalog cabinets will have to be purchased. The same is true of cabinets for the storage of microfilm and other equipment directly related to quantities of material purchased. The continuing need for such purchases is sometimes obscured by the effects of building and equipping new library buildings or extension of old ones. On the whole, however, there is a continuing need for new equipment and for replacement of wornout items. Computer services (in this case, a nominal recovery charge) do not always vary with the quantity of activity undertaken, and the nature of the programs is usually such that the cost will continue roughly the same.

Most budgets include items for miscellaneous expenditure, though this is usually further subdivided by the library. Irregular expenditures for publications (*e.g.*, Union List of Serials), or payment of library memberships will be included. By its nature such a class of expenditure is unpredictable, even though elements within it may be known. Support for travel and research is also unpredictable in detail. Although such expenditure cannot be classed as essential—the library would still survive—it is a highly desirable staff investment and one which has become an integral part of the goals of most libraries.

The purpose of this brief resume is to demonstrate that most expenditures for goods and services are unavoidable. Without the support they provide, the library would cease to function. Each individual library can identify without too much difficulty such continuing expenditures. In the sample budget, the proportion of essential expenditures is on the order of 80 percent. Even that division presumes that travel and research is not essential and that repairs can be postponed indefinitely. If so great a proportion can be established as essential, then inflation will clearly have a great part to play in determining the budgetary requirements for the next and ensuing years. Secondly, the determination of what may be called the "free" proportion establishes equally clearly what nonrecurring expenditure is possible, or what amounts could, if necessary, be transferred to other purposes.

LIBRARY MATERIALS

There are three general classes of expenditure: books, subscriptions and binding. Each class may be defined differently by different libraries. For the purposes of this consideration, books are considered as including all purchases, monographic or otherwise, other than continuing subscriptions. Subscriptions cover periodicals, serials, series, newspapers and long-term microform subscriptions. Binding includes the cost of binding individual monographs, but most of the cost will be for the binding of periodical volumes. The general distribution of library materials costs in the sample budget is shown in Table 4.

Table 4. Library Materials Costs.

Books and other nonsubscription costs	400,000
Periodical and other subscriptions	500,000
Binding	50,000
TOTAL	$950,000

The specific allocations are less important at this stage than the general proportions. The amount allocated to subscriptions (52.63 percent) represents a permanent commitment, as is the case for the minimal binding budget (5.26 percent). Between them, they account for 57.89 percent of the budget for library materials. This expenditure, plus any price increases, will therefore have to be supported in the year being planned for. Only the amounts allocated for books are not, in this sense, fixed. From another perspective, that of the library's goals in collection development, they are fixed, and adjustments between areas may prove hardest to make of all budgetary decisions.

Secondary planning projections can be based on library materials expenditures, since the amount of money available determines the number of items purchased, which in turn determines processing costs and housing requirements. An average, discounted price for books can be derived from fiscal data, or from the various annual price indexes. If this were, for example, $10, then the maximum number of books that could be bought would be 40,000. The total additions to the library's holdings would then consist of this figure plus the number of bound volumes of periodicals. Naturally, the picture is never so clean, since purchases also include maps, microforms, documents, etc., but it is very important to relate the monetary figures to the expected product. Finally, a check against current expenditures in the existing budget will indicate areas of possible over- and under-expenditure. These usually represent differential inflation rates or special opportunities for the purchase of a collection, but may also indicate a change in program resulting from changed academic needs. These differences between planned and actual expenditures should be noted and used in the preparation of the final budget request.

RESERVE OR DISCRETIONARY FUNDS

Not all institutions provide a reserve fund (the technical name will vary according to institutional practice) directly to administrative units. Some prefer to maintain a central fund on the grounds that this allows more planning flexibility. The best practice is, however, to distribute a proportion of such reserve funds to the units, including the library.

Reserve funds are not necessarily permanent in nature, and may include temporary reallocations of money either from within the unit budget or from external sources. It may, for example, be the fund where accounting practice directs savings made on an appointment at a lower figure than the budget allowed, or it may be used as the temporary repository for funds intended for a special purchase which was not made, pending a decision on where those funds should be reallocated. It may also be the fund from which money is drawn to make an appointment at a higher salary than budgeted.

The general intention of a reserve fund is to provide a source for unforeseen expenditures, or for expenditures which by their nature are irregular in occurrence though certain to occur, such as anniversary increases for clerical staff or special temporary appointments. For these reasons, expenditures from a reserve fund may also be permanent or temporary. Given the nature of a library's activities the existence of a reserve fund is critical, since it could provide the resources for the purchase of a highly desirable collection or piece of equipment that could not otherwise be purchased. A review of the disposition of funds during the year will reveal what use has been made of them, and may indicate the likely needs for the coming year.

INCOME

Most libraries have some income from sources such as fines, photoduplication charges, sale of materials, or from the sale of the library's own publications. Internally the library may balance these against the costs incurred in obtaining the income; but, unless a project is set up and funded separately as an enterprise, it is usual for income to be set off against projected expenditure. This distinction is important, since librarians not informed concerning budgetary processes may be under the misapprehension that recorded income is over and above the printed budget. In such a situation the proposal may be made, for example, to discontinue fines, without making provision for appropriate, balancing reductions in expenditure.

The procedures in handling income will differ widely. In some institutions all receipts of income are channeled directly to a central fund; and, in such a case, the individual unit may or may not benefit from higher income than anticipated. A further complication, frequently encountered on the disposition of materials, may be the allocation of that income to a surplus and deficiency account for the year in which the original expenditure was made; which means, in effect, that the library does not receive any of the money, except by application to the responsible administrative officer for a special grant. The nature of the process of acquisition and de-acquisition will usually place the library in such a situation, and the librarian should therefore negotiate, if possible, a special status for the library.

At this stage, the projected income, as shown in the printed budget, should be compared with income received to date and that expected to the end of the year, to determine the reliability of any estimates to be made for the next year.

SUMMARY OF BUDGET ANALYSIS

For use by the library staff concerned, a concise summary of the analysis should be prepared, highlighting areas where there is need for policy decision, or where there are deficits likely unless more money is provided. Summaries of projected expenditures, compared with budget estimates, are helpful in determining the measure of success the library is having in meeting its goals. Information concerning such matters as the relationship between predicated and free funds are also helpful, and Diagram 3 indicates one way in which such information can be presented. Any other information which may be helpful, such as known cost increases, should be included, as should information on vacant positions and known future vacancies. In preparing such a statement, it is necessary to

Diagram 3. Relationship of Predicated Expenditures to Total Budget.

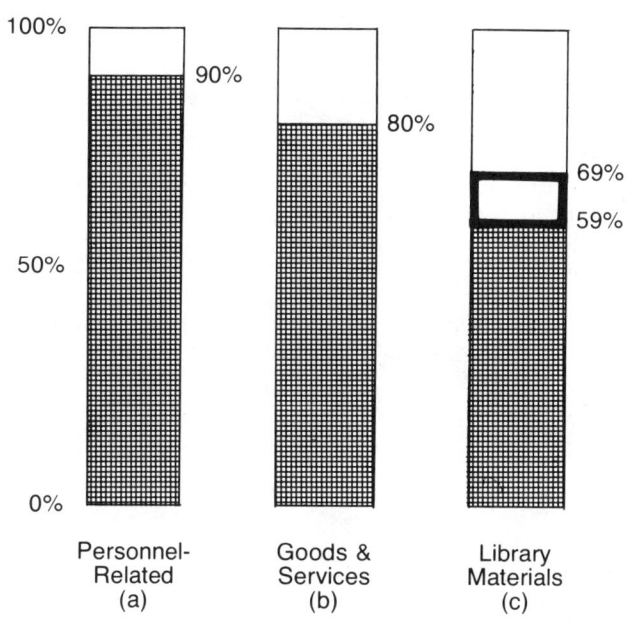

(a) This presumes that a proportion of wage expenditure is unplanned at the beginning of the fiscal year. If there were no resignations or dismissals, all the rest would be spent for existing personnel.

(b) Most unpredicated expenditures are for desirable activities such as travel.

(c) This counts as predicated *only* subscriptions and associated binding; in fact, a further proportion is usually accounted for by outstanding orders or commitments to approval plans which require action by the library to stop. These are represented by the portion of the graph enclosed by a heavy line.

remember that most of the people reading it are not familiar with financial accounts and care must be taken to explain fully what is immediately obvious to the trained accountant.

NOTES

1. The author is indebteded for this categorization of budgets to the work done by Allen (April, 1972) in his report to the Council on Library Resources. See also Robins (1973, pp. 10–14), where a slightly expanded categorization is used.

2. Summers, p. 1177.

3. Thomson (1975, pp. 22–39) makes a very interesting use of FTE student numbers to analyze library expenditures. Its success is, however, the result of the kind of institution being studied.

4. Jeffrey A. Raffel and Robert Shisko, in the course of a study of the Massachusetts Institute of Technology Libraries, carried out a very full analysis of the libraries' expenditures. The tables in the case study given in the appendix suggest the degree of detail required to carry out a cost-benefit analysis.

5. Pings and Spang (1971).

6. Raffel and Shisko (1969).

7. Rogers and Weber (1971), pp. 100–102.

8. Baumol and Marcus (1973), pp. 45–52.

Chapter 5

Collection of Information in Support of a Budget Request

> *With a leveling off of funding for higher education despite increased enrollments, the pressure to account for each available dollar through some kind of performance measurement will undoubtedly increase. . . . The people whose responsibility it is to provide the money are beginning to demand facts, not "self evident truths". . . . What is now being asked of us by outside agencies is, in reality, only what we should be asking ourselves.* (Axford.)

The most necessary information is the knowledge of what information is, in fact, required. This may seem a truism, but it is exceedingly easy to collect information which, however valuable for other purposes such as management, may be useless in terms of a budget request. The instructions accompanying the budget request will usually require explicitly certain kinds of information, but they may also state explicitly what is *not* required. For example, the instructions may require supporting evidence to accompany requests based on increasing programs (*i.e.*, more books purchased per year) but state that inflation is not to be allowed for. In such an instance, of course, while central funds may be provided to counter inflation, if the library suffers greater inflation than the rest of the institution this should be pointed out, but a request to cover basic inflation should not be made. A third category of information may be considered implicit (*i.e.*, if there are expanded academic programs, the library may need more books, though this program expansion was not planned by the library itself), and the library administrator will have to exercise judgement in determining what to say, and what facts to present in support of the request.

Any program budgeting, however simplified, requires the presentation of some kind of analysis of work load as a justification for the budget requested. Few institutions employ a total PPBS approach, and those which do follow the usual pattern of politics in allowing for exceptions. A useful discussion of the complexities in this approach is provided by H. William Axford.[1] A different kind of approach is inherent in the formula budget. The most cogent consideration of this technique is presented in the document concerned with its application in the State of Washington.[2] The analysis presented by Kenneth S. Allen in his study for the Council on Library Resources should be read by all who are concerned with the budget process. Setting out, as it does, the limitations and benefits of formula budgeting, it provides the library administrator with useful comments and questions, and suggests the caution necessary in utilizing any budgetary system.

While the battle still rages over the applicability of performance budgeting to academia, economic realities are moving even those most opposed to it toward some system in which the fate of academic programs is not left entirely to the "clout" of an administrator.

The first question to be asked is what is the library getting for its money? Some of this is revealed by the traditional statistics—number of volumes acquired, number of book circulated, number of reference questions answered, number of interlibrary loans. These are all valid measures of activity; but, in a large library, they do not go nearly far enough to allow the librarian to answer the second question, how well is the money being spent? To investigate alternative patterns requires far greater analysis than these gross figures provide.

Librarians should not feel constrained in the kinds of statistics they keep. The traditional figures presented in annual reports are seldom enough for a real analysis of activity, and may fail entirely to reflect an innovative and highly successful program. The parent institution may also require information outside the statistical mainstream. Certainly libraries must record the information asked for by associations or government agenices, but they need to go beyond this in order to establish the work loads, trends and internal relationships so necessary for planning. If, for example, a new approach to basic English has altered the entire activity of the reference department, the figures must be available to show what has happened, why it happened and what is needed.

Immediately, the objection will be raised that there are no standards which will allow one library to measure its activities and come to any conclusion about their value. As a statement of fact that is correct. Existing standards[3] deal in very broad terms and require detailed interpretation if they are to become meaningful. Nevertheless, these documents, together with referential data from comparable libraries, can provide a useful stimulus toward examining areas of apparent deficiency and determining the reasons for their existence. The most useful figures, however, derive from the activities of the library itself, even more for identification of trends than for the absolute figures. While it is hard to quantify, say, reference questions in terms of staff time in the absence of any generally accepted national performance norms, it is possible to see what changes in level are evident from year to year.

Accepting then the challenge to approach budget preparation from an analytical viewpoint, the library administrator will be concerned to identify critical areas of activity and to group these in a fashion which enables them to be linked with a budget request. This kind of approach, incidentally, applies whether the budget is to be increased, decreased or remain the same. It also has the merit of similarity to the use of student credit-hours as a measure of academic activity. Such a rationale is the basis of most formula or program budgets. It is, important, however, not to be caught in the tyranny of figures, particularly because all formulae are at once subjective and empirical. As with most academic activities it is impossible to assign quantitative values to qualitative services. How much is a reference question worth? It takes its worth from its context, and as this context may change, so may the worth of the question. Such relativism is difficult to translate into the cold terms desired by the budgetary process; and despite themselves, therefore, librarians must offer quantitative measurements but must use these measurements as sensitively as possible. To use the conclusion of Peter Drucker's speech at an ACRL meeting:

> In other words, if librarian/administrators do not know their publics and respond to their needs, if they do not know their institutions and make a visible impact with their programs, people who deal in figures will determine the future of our libraries.[4]

To counteract those nonlibrarians who deal in figures, librarians need to use those same figures effectively in support of their own goals.

If, of course, there is no consensus on the library's goals, then it is extremely difficult to justify them; hence the need, greatly stressed in recent library literature, for a clear statement of goals. What is implied by Drucker, and, from a different perspective, by Axford is the need for libraries to assess their role within the institution, in consultation with the academic community, in order to demonstrate support for the role in a more realistic way than by reference to generalized, ideal standards.

A final influence on the statistics that are required is the framework within which the institutional budget is conceived. It may for example, require the use of book/student ratios or comparison of holdings to an ideal table of volume equivalents, or the use of a staff/student ratio in the determination of Public-service staff numbers. All such requirements have a rigidity which may require of the administrator that he insist on exceptions to provide for the unique situation. Such formulae (more correctly their mechanistic application) simplify the judgemental activities of the assessor, but may easily wreak havoc in a library caught in a downward financial spiral, because they are unable to take into account such factors as inertia, inequitable distribution of inflation or the need for different economic responses from different units. All these and more must be the concern of the administrator as he seeks to describe and to justify the library and its activities.

The concept of inertia is an important one for libraries. In physics, inertia is that property of matter by which it continues in a state of rest or of uniform motion unless that state is changed by external force. Its application to libraries is obvious. When an item is purchased, if it is to be made available for use, various kinds of processes have to be carried out before it can end up on the shelf. Equally ineluctably material purchased will have to be housed. Unless some major policy change is initiated this process will continue, since it is one of the basic purposes of a library. Its existence will therefore have major effects on any budgetary proposals. The time and the cost consumed by the application of the necessary force may be exemplified by the changes effected in a library by the adoption of the Ohio College Library Center as a source of cataloging. Because most of the changes made—collapsing positions, buying equipment, transfer of card-stock purchase money from supplies to services—are irreversible, a new inertial force is set up in the library which will widen its effects as the new program expands and deepens. Understanding the meaning of such forces is essential to the success of forward planning. Otherwise, provision may not be made for essential costs, and costly changes may have to be made interfering with other operations. Looked at another way, inertia is a kind of continuity; and within the academic community libraries are the unit most dependent on continuity for the satisfactory provision of their services to that community.

The information collected must ensure that the necessary consequences of all policy decisions are accounted for. Strange as it may seem, this is not always the case. For example, there is frequently pressure from faculty, students or central administration to extend the hours of library opening. It usually comes as a shock to the requester to be told that there is a cost associated with such an action—whether in the form of added costs for more staff hours or in the more subtle and more dangerous form of other activities not undertaken.

Generalized statements cannot cover individual cases. Nevertheless the following categories of activity are common to all libraries: the acquisition and cataloging of library materials, the circulation of those materials and reference and allied services. Each of these can be further subdivided, depending largely on the organization of the library. Certain activities stand outside these categories, but bear on overhead relationship. Examples would be automation and administration. The requirement then is to gather appropriate information to support a budget request which responds to demonstrated need. The form in which this information is then presented is controlled by the instructions supplied by the administration.

Each category of activity should be analyzed for factors which may demonstrate different patterns of change. The factors used in establishing the budget for the Pennsylvania State University Libraries provide an example of such an analysis. (See Table 5.) In the modified PPBS approach used in that institution, work-load activity analysis factors were assigned to all academic or administrative units, less to derive standard unit costs, than to encourage the standardization of data and its presentation and to provide some means of measuring or estimating trends. Although the number of such factors available to the libraries was arbitrarily limited to seven, it was found possible within these limits to place almost all library activities. Before summarizing them, it is, however, necessary to stress that these factors are not in themselves budget determinants, but rather signs which assist the administration in making decisions.

It is not suggested that this particular number or combination of factors would be suitable for all libraries.[5] A similar analytical mode was employed by Pings at Wayne State University, where the number of activity categories was six. In the absence, however, of generally accepted definitions and categories of library work, libraries which wish to go beyond the traditional statistics will have to adopt some similar method for the measuring of work loads. The categories presented in Table 5 are designed to permit the incorporation of all independent activities; hence, there is no direct representation of cataloging, or of accounting, since these will vary with the acquisitions program. Such dependent variables are

Table 5. Workload-activity Indicators Used at the Pennsylvania State University.

(a) *Volumes added* (Code 091): Number of monographs, serials, microforms, maps, documents, etc., added to the collection. *Factors included:* Number of orders received, number of orders placed, number of volumes received, number of periodical parts received, number of volumes bound, and number of replacements ordered.

(b) *Collection usage* (Code 092): Total number of volumes issued to patrons, including closed reserve volumes and periodicals issued, and resulting activities, plus total use measured by materials reshelved in the stacks. *Other factors:* Number of personal reserves made, number of overdues sent out/fine notices, and number of items transferred to reserve.

(c) *Catalogue maintenance* (Code 093): Number of cards filed in public and other catalogs, number of cards withdrawn. *Factors included:* Number of new cards filed, number of old cards withdrawn, catalogs/shelf-lists/authority files/serials Acme.

(d) *Reclassifications* (Code 094): Number of volumes transferred from Dewey Decimal to Library of Congress classification.

(e) *Facilities usage* (Code 095): Count of all patrons leaving the library.

(f) *Reference services* (Code 096): Number of questions, number of bibliographies and booklists prepared, number of orientational and instructional services given.

(g) *Interlibrary Loans* (Code 097): Number of interlibrary loans and other questions handled.

(h) *Weighted library SVC units* (Code 098): Overall calculated workload indicator, to be calculated from above indicators, using formula shown below:

Indicator #901 times 4.00=_____
Indicator #092 times 0.10=_____
Indicator #093 times 0.05=_____
Indicator #094 times 3.00=_____
Indicator #096 times 4.00=_____
Indicator #097 times 3.00=_____

_____

Indicator #098 (sum of above)_____

covered by the system of weighting. The rationale for this kind of grouping can best be explained by the examination of one indicator: Collection Usage. The common statistical report in this area is the total number of volumes circulated, which might at first glance appear perfectly adequate, and would be so, if all other activities varied in harmony with the circulation figures. In fact, they do not. The reasons for this independent variability are many: changes in policy or charges may restrict circulation but increase use in-house; social changes in study habit may bring more students into the library, though they may not borrow more; a change in procedure may transfer a count from one activity to another without the proponent's being aware of it; it may become impossible to handle as many personal reserves; or there may be an increase in the amount of material transferred to the reserve collection. Each of these changes may affect a number of library activities differently. To take a hypothetical example, the number of books actually circulated may remain the same, say, 500,000; but the number of books used in the library and reshelved may rise from 400,000 to 800,000, while the numbers of requests for the photocopying of library materials may decline from 250,000 to 200,000. If only circulation figures were used, there would be no apparent change in work load, whereas in fact the work load increased from 1,150,000 to 1,500,000 transactions, an increase of about 30 percent.

It is true that norms are not presently available that would enable any set of figures to be converted into staff requirements. The absence of such norms should not, however, prevent librarians from developing measurements for their own libraries. As pointed out by Sarah Thomson, "valid and reliable means of measuring are essential before meaningful standards can be written."[6] If librarians do not try to measure, they may never arrive at standards which are more than platitudinous. Until, however, such nationally accepted standards are available to provide a measure, any analysis of work load can only be used to determine trends, or to examine changes, whether of activity or productivity, within the institution. Such trends may be seen within each group of activities or between activities,[7] and these are the kinds of facts and figures required by administrations.

A second class of information concerns the institution itself. Information is usually available concerning student enrollments, credit-hours and number of faculty. Not all administrators recognize how important such information is to libraries. The library administrator should make it his goal to have all information of this kind available. Not only are absolute numbers important, but their distribution. For example, the needs of a student body of 10,000, but which includes 3,000 graduate students, will differ greatly from a similar sized body which includes only 500 graduate students. Academic distribution is also important, particularly in heavily book-dependent areas such as the humanitities.

Care must be taken, however, to avoid the pitfalls of some formula budgets in which the size of the budget is related directly to enrollment. While this may be true for such programs as reserve books, it must be stressed that a more important determinant for libraries is the number of academic programs at the institution. The support needs of a program are affected only marginally by the number of students. Information should therefore be collected concerning new academic programs or changes in existing ones. Ideally the library should be involved in all academic planning, and library needs should be taken into consideration. Unfortunately, this is seldom the case. Whether or not the library has had an opportunity to participate in planning, it is essential to keep a record of new courses and new programs or changes in either.

Information on academic programs, student enrollments, research projects and number of faculty should be drawn together into an academic profile of the institution. In the absence of any other indication, it may be presumed that this profile represents the investment that society, as mediated through the organizational structure of the institution, is willing to make in the institution. There is not always an exact parallel: for example, it may take time to trim the faculty in a discipline which no longer receives strong social support, witnessed by declining student enrollment. Equally, since academia does not (and should not) always follow current whims, certain unpopular disciplines, such as the classics or the language departments, may be retained despite their unpopularity, because they are a necessary part of the wholeness of knowledge.

In summary then, at this stage in the process, the library administrator will have:

(1.) an analysis of present library expenditures;
(2.) an analysis of present library activities;
(3.) an academic analysis of the institution.

Although it has been necessary here to treat the recovery of these analyses as part of the preparation for a budget presentation, they will, of course, be matters of constant concern to the library administrator and should therefore be available at the proper time without great additional effort. If the proper records are kept, it should only be necessary to assemble the information in the proper form. It cannot be stressed enough that effective management requires effective access to, and use of, information.

CONSULTATION

The budget officer or library adminstrator who has struggled with the information flow considered in the preceding section frequently feels that he knows enough to proceed directly into budget preparation. Such a feeling, though apparently justified, if only by the sweat of one's brow, is a cardinal sin to which the financially adept are prone. Nothing could be further from the truth. All data are meaningful only when interpreted. The interpretation of one person is seldom adequate. While it may emerge little changed from a long series of considerations by others, such a testing adds to its strength.

The process of evaluation by consultation is usually a harrowing one. No easy rules can be set up to govern it. Each case must establish its own guidelines. A budget request in which one may ask for more is clearly quite different from one in which a certain decrease must be made. What is required is, basically, that the facts arrived at in the course of information gathering be presented to the appropriate segment of the library staff, their reactions and suggestions sought and a budget request be based on the resulting discussion. Such discussion must be under the control of the library administration, which will recognize this process for what it is, a political one.

The length, depth and range of the discussion must to some extent be controlled by the guidelines of the institution. Usually there is a finite time within which the budget request must be prepared. This might, in earlier years, have been predictable, but, as money has become tighter is an uncertain economy, legislatures or boards of trustees have frequently found themselves unable to continue within established patterns, so that either the time for presentation has crept forward or supplementary budget actions far from being the exception have become the rule. The only way to overcome this uncertainty of timing is to be prepared at all times. That may seem to many an unnecessary chore, but it is the only way in which an intelligent response to a budget request can be prepared in three weeks. This implies that department heads, or a budget advisory committee, if such is in existence, should meet regularly to consider the financial aspects of the library's operations.

Whatever process is used, library units must themselves be given guidelines within which to present their requests. These guidelines will naturally reflect the institution's own guidelines. If, for example, the institution has not planned for new permanent positions, the library is unlikely to be able to provide any unless by cannibalization. The instructions must therefore be realistic and couched in terms that are easily understandable. The specialized terms used by accountants are seldom readily understood by librarians and therefore require expansion and explanation; yet care must be taken not to lose the precision implicit in such terms. For example, accounts receivable as a class includes credit notes. These are actually debts owed to the library, generated perhaps by returned books or by sales of duplicates. They may be used to offset future expenditures and are in this sense income, since they extend the purchasing power of the library, whether or not they also represent a reimbursement of part or all of a previous payment. As income, they should be included in the forward estimate of income for the next year, an estimate which is based in part on experience. Many librarians, however, persist in regarding such credits as a kind of bonus, whose exclusive use they claim. Simply to include accounts receivable in the budget would not provide an explanation. Instead, the explanation given above is necessary, or even individual discussion with those most affected.

It is obviously necessary to make clear the limitations imposed by the institution. If it is possible, each unit head should receive a statement couched in terms that relate directly to that unit, although general advice on library needs and priorities may also be sought. Matters which should be required are:

(1) present activities, accompanied by relevant data;
(2) likely growth of activity, accompanied by support data, and information on such matters as increased costs;
(3) resources required to meet the growth in activity;
(4) alternative courses if these resources cannot be made available, including a statement of priorities;
(5) relationship of unit request to library-wide goals.

This request for a budget submission should be accompanied by the analysis of the library's activities and budget capacity. The route by which it is sent out and returned will be determined by the library's organization, but as a general principle all such requests should be forwarded via any superior officer, who should in turn be required to comment upon the request. All responses to requests should, however, be returned to the officer directly responsible for budget preparation, to ensure that they are available for consideration.

The budget officer should assemble these requests and check them against existing information and statistics to ensure both accuracy and completeness. Discrepancies should be checked out with the unit concerned and a reconciliation be made. Lack of time frequently compresses this process to the point that consultation can only be minimal, but it is essential that some feedback be provided, before decisions are made as well as after. It is equally important that discussion at this level be factual and impartial. Any suggestion of approval of or agreement with a unit's needs can only lead to dissension since it will be perceived as favoritism by others not so treated or, if the apparent promise is not kept, failure to keep it will be regarded as a kind of betrayal.

In any presentation to the library administration, however, the budget officer must indicate his assessment of the proposals submitted. Particular attention must be paid to whether the costs are realistic, to whether any have been omitted, or exaggerated, and to the effect of the proposal on other units. The relationship to the library's goals and objectives should also be examined and priorities assigned in keeping with these relationships. At this stage, initial information gathering is complete, and the process of decision-making begins.

NOTES
1. Axford, pp. 87–104.
2. Allen (1972), Appendix A.
3. "Standards for College Libraries" (October 1975), pp. 277–279, 290–300. Other guidelines are referred to in this issue of the *College and Research Libraries News*. The explanatory matter accompanying the standards deserves the closest examination by all librarians.
4. "Report on Peter Drucker's Speech," *College and Research Library News,* No. 8, September 1975, p. 264.
5. David Palmer, in "Measuring Library Output," quoted by Harold Jenkins, points out that comparative statistics are not too helpful, and that librarians should be prepared to keep any statistics which can be used to demonstrate need.
6. Thomson (1975), p. 141.
7. LeMoyne Anderson, in his paper "New Dynamics of Research Libraries and Networks," presented at the 88th meeting of the Association of Research Libraries, cites trends in library use which run counter to other observed conditions. His remarks on the difficulties of measuring are well-taken.

Chapter 6

The Use of Statistics to Support a Budget Request

> *Anybody who has ever negotiated with administrators, trustees, and state budget directors knows that they are not impressed by vague "guidelines" . . . These practical men and women want to know what an authoritative body of experts considers essential; they insist on facts and figures.*
> (Hirsch.)

All the information in the world will not guarantee the preparation of a successsful budget request. Much, if not most, of its success will depend upon the care with which the information concerning facts and figures is assembled and articulated. Even the most obstinate of formulae are amenable to change, if the case can be made cogently enough. It is at this stage, when the information is all in, that the interplay of political and economic decision-making becomes all-important.

How this discussion and decision-making should be carried out is beyond the scope of this study. A useful preparatory consideration of this problem is provided by Raffel, who suggests some of the political needs now beginning to surface in libraries.[1] It is, however, essential to realize the importance of the political aspect. In reference to a PPB system; Kenneth S. Allen puts his finger on the reason for consultation.

> One of the significant problems here is the ability, or lack of it, to isolate programs and alternatives to a point where the judgements can be based upon common quantitative criteria. Most frequently the program in question and the alternatives cannot stand alone but are affected by, or affect, other programs in the overall university scheme.[2]

Although this statement is directed toward budgeting for the institution as a whole, it is equally true of the academic library. Not only must the library take into account the external programs that it is required to support but also the relationships of its internal programs to one another and to those external programs. In recognizing the need to allow internal program planners to participate in the library's budget process, the library administrator must also recognize that this decision has called into being at a lower level the advocacy, controversy and special pleading which already accompanies the allocation of finances at higher levels in the institution. Such a method of operation requires a strong monitor or control system for balance, which is the role of the fact-gathering and analysis described in Chapter 4. It provides a framework against which to measure the various program proposals submitted by the units within the library.

The procedures used in preparing a budget request will vary according to the priorities and the instructions contained in the budget instructions. At some time in the process, however, the unit heads, who were requested to present a statement of their needs and expectations, should be given a chance to defend that request, or, at the least, be informed of decisions. It is necessary to identify the parts of the budget appropriate to each unit head so that it is clear what resources will be purchased and to demonstrate how those purchases will be used to produce the desired service products, the whole articulated in such a way as to make it clear that consideration has been given both to individual and to collective goals. This exercise is made much easier if individual unit heads have earlier been involved in the budgetary process.

Most librarians have spent their professional lives in a work situation where the incremental budget has been the rule. Such a budget seeks to maintain old programs and to expand gradually by widening existing programs or introducing new ones. In this they have been following a political model which sought to maximize user (*i.e.*, voter) pleasure. Faced with a situation in which such incrementalism is no longer possible, many have retreated into a defensive position, trying to hold what belongs to the unit and to prevent others from taking anything away. This is frequently rationalized as the maintenance of successful programs or the keeping up of needed services, and there is sufficient truth in both these claims to make very difficult any radical changes in the allocation of resources. The first objective of any budget presentation within the library is to help unit heads transcend this defensiveness by encouraging them to see the part each unit must play within the library as a whole in meeting the new demands. No matter how well it may be received by higher administrative levels, a budget which is forced upon those who must work with it will have only limited effectiveness. While the blessings which are seen by William Summers[3] to flow from the use of a PPBS approach seem exaggerated, participation in budget-making *is* an educative process. If this is borne firmly in mind, the library administrator will find it easier to handle discussions and planning sessions. In certain circumstances, such as a reduced budget, it may be necessary to refuse all requests for extra funds or to divert funds to the maintenance of operations basic to the library. This sort of decision, while it appears self-evident, requires explanation. It also requires the cooperation and support of all who are involved, if it is to be effective.

Decision-making of this kind cannot be made solely by majority vote since the implementation of the results must be the responsibility of the administrators concerned. A representative consultative committee may properly consider all aspects of the budget and prepare recommendations for the library administration. Discussion of alternatives with such a group will help clarify the issues involved. To them should be presented the various proposals, together with costs and other contextual information. From such a discussion should emerge a more realistic appraisal of the proposed changes and a better developed sense of priorities.

It is at this point that agreement on the library's short- and long-term goals assumes critical importance. These will differ with the general financial situation. Where the absolute priority is to survive, desirable but nonessential proposals must take second place, while services such as circulation are maintained. In a freer financial environment more latitude is allowable, though even then each proposal must be examined for its impact on other library programs and services.

Two situations based on the sample library may help render this concept more understandable. For the past two years the circulation figures have shown an 8 percent rate of increase. Last year the increase was absorbed by the existing staff, but the lending service librarian now advises the library administration that the staff is having difficulty in ensuring rapid filing of cards and reshelving of books, while still attempting to keep track of overdues and personal reserves. An activity audit is under way in the hope of simplifying some routines, but this is not expected materially to improve the staff/workload ratio beyond the point where they can cope better with the present load. The librarian is requesting two extra clerks and an addition to the wage payroll to handle end-of-term loads. The reported statistics appear to substantiate the claim and the personnel officer confirms the lowered state of morale. In the circumstances the request appears self-justifying. The budget distribution, however, shows the following staff:

    2 professional
    3 semiprofessionals
   14 clericals
    8 FTE wage personnel ($40,000)

Of this number, three are assigned full-time to interlibrary loan and two to photoduplication, while three spend most of their time at the exit desk where they check outgoing materials. In fact, therefore, eight of the staff of nineteen are not engaged in circulation activities *per se*. The lion's share of these activities is borne by one semiprofessional and eight clerks together with the 8 FTE provided by wage expenditure. A simple increase of 8 percent in work load, presuming there are no adjustments that can be made in procedures or assignments, would justify one more full-time person and additional wages. Discussion reveals that, in fact, problems have arisen over assignment of part-time help to photoduplication; and the real intention behind the request for extra personnel was to remove one source of friction. No formula, no program, no analysis can solve such a problem, nor can it easily be built into the rationale supporting a budget request; but these are in fact the kinds of problems that may be solved by the successful handling of the budgetary process. In this case a reasonable solution might require some reassignment of responsibilities (which is a management problem internal to the department) and the addition of one full-time staff member on the basis of an increased work load. Whether in fact this is done will depend on a great many other factors, but the case is cited as a very simple example of primary analysis, which can serve as a basis for later decisions when the final budget request is being shaped. What is required is that all requests be related in some quantitative way to programs, and to their objectives—in this case to provide a quicker turn-round time for circulated materials, which is a primary goal of the library.

A more complex issue is raised by the situation in which there is pressure to provide a new service, in this case reference and acquisitions support for a new academic program. Failure to build in such library support is perhaps the problem most often mentioned by librarians, who have, nevertheless, generally managed to squeeze together enough money to provide some resources, a response which is the equivalent of cutting one's own throat to provide someone else with a blood transfusion. The most sensible procedure, but one seldom followed, would have been for the insitution's administration to have consulted the library in the course of establishing the new program and to have provided the necessary funds for setting up library support. In the more usual procedure the fact of the program's establishment is used as a reason why the library should reallocate existing resources to support it. Any rational economic analysis would simply provide a negative reply, but politically it is inevitable that some service will be given "for the sake of the student." In such a situation the library administrator can see only that no more resources are so reallocated than the bare minimum required, unless the parent administration is willing and able to provide fully funded support. It is not an ideal solution, but it is the most likely one.

If the program is to be developed, the necessary consequence is the consideration of the range of resources which must be reallocated. If, for example, the program is one in Far Eastern studies, the impact is likely to be more wide-ranging, than if it is, say, an extension of the Spanish program into Portuguese. The effects on selection, acquisition, cataloging, reference and stack maintenance must all be considered in arriving at a program cost. A shopping list that represents the true costs in the establishment of a library support program is seldom greeted with either enthusiasm or belief, even when it is accompanied by references to standards or comparative statistics. Reaction *post hoc* is clearly, therefore, even more difficult. Some formula budgets would provide funds for materials, but would be unlikely to make possible the hiring of expensive specialists. In the situation where a new program is begun and an old one terminated, a formula budget would not even provide funds for materials, no matter how unrelated the new subject matter is to the existing collections. To put the matter very simply, even to provide 1,000 books in support of the program will require a minimum expenditure of $10,000, to which must be added the costs of processing which, depending on the standard costs assumed, will vary between $5,000 and $10,000 (perhaps even reaching $15,000 in the case of the Far Eastern example), and the costs of moving materials to provide shelf space in the proper location. The latter is by no means negligible if, as may well be the case, a substantial number of other books must be moved to allow for the location of 1,000 books in the ten bays of shelving required, in their proper sequence, among the collections. Such problems, incidentally, are frequently the reason for cost overruns in the stack maintenance department. Even now, the appropriate public service must be allowed for, which might be a half-time librarian at an annual salary of $14,000. The rest of the time is presumed to be spent on acquisitions, cataloging or other library activities. Thus, even to make a relatively modest investment in a new program, the library must receive in new funds or take from other programs a total amount of not less than $22,000 and possibly more than $33,000—the most important fact concerning which is that, by its nature, it becomes a permanent commitment.

The first round of consideration then is given to individual proposals to arrive at some kind of ordinal sequence, so that they may then be measured against budget capabilities and the general requirements of maintaining existing programs. In this stage of analysis the aim is to provide efficient resource allocation to meet the goals and objectives of the library. To achieve this aim it is necessary to avoid the several common errors well described by John Keller: "One is ignorance of, or the overlooking of, a better alternative for accomplishing an objective," an error frequently caused by bias. "A second . . . is the pursuit of the wrong object," which frequently means that the wrong questions are asked and the wrong answers are provided as the basis for resource allocation. Third is the "pursuit of the right objective but beyond some reasonable point of diminishing returns," which may perhaps most easily be typified by overinvestment in a particular segment of the collections which is now receiving very little use. The fourth is "the failure to recognize all the costs involved in an alternative."[4] Each of the proposals cited earlier illustrates one or more of these errors.

The core decision-group must then assess both general and specific needs. The procedure will differ according to the response required by the institution. If a formula budget is followed, it will be necessary to calculate the required figures and align these with the present distribution of resources, remembering that in most formulae there are special areas not covered for which special, separate requests must be made. For any of the program types of budget, calculations of the factors involved will be required, together with projections of program expectations. The traditional or object budget is the simplest to handle, but the accretional objects must themselves be ranked and analyzed for effect. Given this diversity of approach, it is nearly impossible to suggest a general methodology, other than to stress the need for accuracy in the estimation of costs and the need to compare like things.

In the sample case that is being used, the modified program approach requires several actions. The first is to project the necessary indicators. These are derived from the statistics maintained by the various units, which were supplied along with the budget requests. In developing these indicators, two things must be remembered. First, as with formulae, the generalized groupings are meaningful only in gross terms. They establish trends or likely totals which can be incorporated into the institutional presentation. Second, the detailed allocation must still be made, internally, in response to specific needs within the library. Provided that the temptation is resisted to regard these figures as having absolute rather than relative values, they can be used as predictors, either singly or interactively. As the time sequence extends, the figures and the predictions can be refined. Finally, they can provide excellent ammunition when the librarian is required to show what is being done with money provided.[5]

From the very simplified projections in Table 6 one may deduce that inflation (or lack of money) is holding down the growth of the collection. As an understandable corollary the use of interlibrary loans is increasing rapidly. The use of the building is increasing relatively slowly, but use of the collection is projected to increase substantially, following the pattern already revealed in reference services provided. Because these figures represent very gross groupings of activities, they cannot provide the necessary detail in support of a specific request. They can and do present a general

Table 6. Projection of Activity Indicators.

	Previous Year	Current Year	Projection
Collection Growth:	80,000	75,000	70,000
Collection Usage:	1,050,00	1,150,000	1,500,000
Facilities Usage:	800,000	850,000	900,000
Reference Services:	300,000	400,000	450,000
Interlibrary Loan:	20,000	25,000	30,000

70 / *Budgetary Control in Academic Libraries*

Diagram 4. Trends in Activity Indicators (Base = 100).

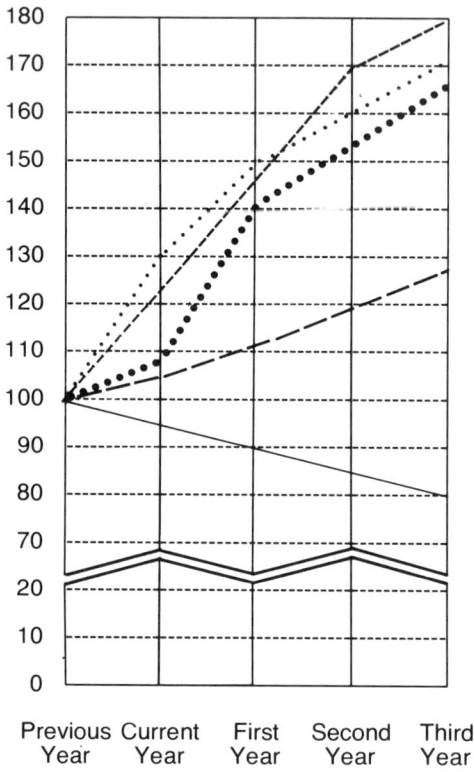

Collection Growth ─────────
Collection Usage ••••••••••••••••
Facilities Usage ── ── ── ──
Reference Services ················
Interlibrary Loan ----------------

picture as a background against which to measure particular growth and specific need. It is important to remember that they are not directly cost-related. An interlibrary loan transaction costs a great deal more than one circulation of a book, even though each has brought together one reader and one book. Similarly, the combination of staff needed within each group of transactions will vary greatly. It is, therefore, necessary in using any trend indicators to analyze them as finely as is necessary to support the library's budget request.

. Here one frequently runs into the objection that academic activities cannot be quantified or evaluated. In a large sense that is true, but is must not be allowed to obscure the fact that all activities have a cost and budgets are concerned with costs. Changes in quantities of activities performed change the cost of the operation. Libraries should, therefore, know how much work is being done and of what kind. The direction and magnitude of growth should also be known. If it is possible to say that directional questions have increased 50 percent, while reference questions (*i.e.*, requiring more than 15 minutes of staff time) have increased 10 percent and research questions (*i.e.*, requiring one hour and more of time) have increased 15 percent, these statements say something not only about the growth being experienced but about the resources needed to respond to that growth. First, of course, this particular set of figures must be put in context. Are these long-term trends or are they the result of special circumstances, such as a move to a new building, in the case of directional questions, or perhaps the provision of access to data bases, in the case of research questions? It is also important to determine what proportion of the total activity each accounts for. Percentages or index charts can easily obscure the fact that only a miniscule portion of whatever universe is being discussed is affected by whatever change is so represented. Within the confines of our sample library this may be illustrated by the changes in reference services provided.

The trends shown in Table 7 indicate a fairly consistent pattern over time. The large jump in directional questions in the current year reflects changes both in services and layout.Although there is heavy pressure for research services, future growth is expected to be limited by lack of staff-time and by the effects of the cost-recovery changes necessary to continue data-base searching services. In such a context then, the relatively small numerical increase in research questions represents a much more substantial library investment than the much larger increase in directional questions. The impact of the increase is reinforced by its concentration in two or three service areas in contradistinction to the very wide dispersal of directional questions through nearly all units of the library.

Table 7. Changes in Reference Services.

	Previous Years	Current Year	Next Year
Directional Questions	168,000	252,000	286,000
Reference Questions	90,000	99,000	110,000
Research Questions	42,000	49,000	54,000
TOTAL	300,000	400,000	450,000

For these reasons a decision has already been made to limit the expansion of research services, notably by requiring total cost recovery for data-base searches. No policy of limitation can, of course, be completely enforced in an academic setting, since much of the effectiveness of library service depends on the willingness of the librarians to go beyond a basic commitment; and in the long run it is usually a matter of slowing down response-time rather than of refusing services outright.

Prediction of the future is, therefore, extremely difficult now and will remain so, even when standards are made available for measuring reference and other public services. The best that can be presented is an intelligible summary of present activities and a thoughtful estimate of future trends. In that future, some indication must also be given of what priority such services will have, while at the same time stressing that the controls that any library may exert are, in the nature of things, very limited. The results of this lack of internal control vary greatly, reflecting almost directly the general budgetary climate. When money is freely available, services are expanded with little attempt to analyze or control that expansion. When money is in short supply, *ad hoc* substitutional changes are the most common response. Neither of these actions is necessarily paralleled by the reactions of the academic community. Indeed there is some evidence that library use intensifies in uncertain economic times. Care must, of course, be taken in the interpretation of trends, especially since there is no universally accepted model and no body of behavioral theory which can be used to support such a case.

A final grouping of information must be assembled. The grouping comprises appropriate documentation from existing standards, or comparative statistics. As pointed out by Felix E. Hirsch, these cannot be references to "vague" guidelines, they must be "what an authoritative body of experts considers essential."[6] They must also be realistic. No matter what a set of standards may say, if the result is so far removed from the present state as to be unattainable without great expenditures, the bold presentation of such standards may have a harmful effect. Equally, care must be taken to select other colleges or universities whose goals, size and style are comparable. This is not to say that for emphasis it may not be useful to quote from a Harvard annual report a discussion on the impossibility of achieving all goals simultaneously,[7] but it is clearly impossible to draw useful parallels for the establishment of budget needs at a small four-year liberal arts college. Comparative statistics are difficult to handle and any conclusions can be only tentative—partly because there is no norm against which they can be measured, but mostly because each library's statistics refer to a unique situation. They can be used to illustrate great differences, say, in the size of the collections, or to show trends among comparable libraries, but in the long run they can be no more than a marginal asset. As David Palmer puts it:

> For the purpose of PPBS, don't rely on statistics which are designed to compare your library with another library.[8]

What is needed is something to reinforce the lesson of the library's own statistics. The goal is not simply to emulate another library but to show how other libraries are responding to similar service requirements. This can in turn be used to show how the library intends to use further resources to provide services.

NOTES
1. Raffel, pp. 412–423.
2. Allen (1972), p. 14.
3. Summers, p. 1180.
4. Keller, pp. 157–158.
5. H. William Axford, commenting on the Report to ARL of The Committee on University Library Standards, said, "I have never seen any yet that had anything there that would be a different type of standard, and that would be a performance standard in the sense of how well are libraries using what resources have been and will be allocated to them." (Association of Research Libraries, *National Perspectives for ARL Libraries, Minutes of the 68th meeting,* Washington, D.C., 1975. p. 43.) Indicators are but a very tentative step toward such measurements and their more effective use awaits the formulation of just such standards.
6. Hirsch, p. 161.
7. Harvard University Library's *Annual Report for the Year 1973–1974,* p. 2.
8. David Palmer, quoted by Harold Jenkins in *Toward an Assessment of Academic Library Organization Effectiveness,* p. 45.

Chapter 7

Budgetary and Economic Restraints and the Setting of Priorities

> *Most members of the University community already are aware of the sober financial realities within which the University must do its budget planning.* (Office of Budget and Planning, 1976–1977 Program Budget Planning.)

Despite the continuing financial crisis in higher education, many academics continue unware of the severity of that crisis. The single fact that salaries (mostly for tenured personnel) and fringe benefits may account for 80 percent of an institutional budget should be warning enough. In such a situation, it is clear that other areas must absorb the greater part of any budgetary reductions, and libraries are unfortunately one of those other areas.

It is appropriate at this stage to consider the different problems posed for libraries by the financial situation of the parent institution. Expanding budgets are the exception, but even they have problems. As is clearly evidenced by the uncontrolled growth of the sixties, easy access to money usually prevents an analytical approach to planning. Indeed planning may simply become reactive and preoccupied with specific problems. In that situation questions such as why and how are seldom asked. Alternative methods or solutions are not explored and the stage is set for *ad hoc* response to pressure.

The most serious legacy of the fat years has been a multiplication of service points, each supported in its time by a perfectly logical rationale, the desire to provide better and more personal access to a constantly growing library. When it becomes impossible to maintain all these service points at the level to which the user community has become accustomed, the question of reducing either the number of service points or the services given at them will evoke pained and sometimes incredulous responses from within the library and certainly from the rest of the academic community. Yet the question was always there, hidden by the availability of sufficient funds to maintain the *status quo*. This apparent carelessness of the consequences appears to remain among the academic members of the community; witness their frequently expressed surprise at any suggestion that the number of courses and programs offered should be in any way restricted. Librarians and libraries suffer double jeopardy in any change of financial climate, since, for the most part, the benefits of increased money come late to libraries and the problems of money shortages come early. This paradoxical situation reinforces the need for careful library planning even in fat years, when consideration must be given to the inertial effects of current and previous decisions.

Static budgets present libraries with the very difficult problem of reallocating resources when the situation is not perceived as sufficiently serious to warrant major changes. Nevertheless, in a unit which has been subject for many years to inflationary trends much greater than the average, a static budget is the equivalent of a drastic cut. When, over a period of years, as demonstrated by Baumol and Marcus,[1] it can be seen that library costs have been rising by an average of 4.5 percent a year, simply to maintain a "normal" rate of accession and staff growth, it is clear that the sudden advent of a no-increase budget will send shock waves throughout the system. And this effect is reinforced when it occurs contemporaneously with even more severe inflation in the general economy.

The static budget is perhaps the most difficult to explain to the library staff and to the academic community. Because there has been no actual loss in dollars (perhaps even an increase recording increases in salaries) people do not believe there is any necessity to cut back on individual activities or purchases. Even though it can be demonstrated that simply maintaining basic programs will absorb all the apparent reserves in the budget, the feeling will remain that some other way of dividing the pie would have ensured a larger slice for whoever feels cheated.

Everyone would claim to be aware of the effects of a reduced budget. There is, however, a considerable difference between an intellectual and an actual grasp of the effects. Not only does it mean a scaling down, as in the case of acquisitions, but it will almost certainly require that some programs be eliminated entirely, or the services provided in a completely different way. It will also require that the pattern of expenditure be altered to reflect what must be a new set of priorities. Because libraries do not, in general, control the use that is made of them, services such as lending will continue almost unchanged and will appear to be receiving a rather greater share of the budget when in fact they are simply being maintained. By way of paradox, some special services, such as interlibrary loan, may even increase because of the lower local availability of resources. It is an interesting commentary on the changed economic conditions in libraries that charges for services previously given free should coincide with a period when libraries, and presumably individuals, are less able to pay for those services. In fact, it is a very belated recognition of the fact that every transaction has a cost, but that the library community has never truly made the decision as to who should bear that cost. We may expect, in the next few years, considerably more definite thinking of this matter.

To give these remarks a more concrete frame of reference, the effects on an acquisitions budget may be considered. In our sample library the existing distribution of the library materials budget in Books, $400,000; Periodicals, $500,000; Binding, $50,000. Given that this represents a desirable distribution, the objective of budgetary planning would be to maintain that distribution, whatever the rate of inflation might be. In general terms, if inflation averages 15 percent, a year. in the first year a further $142,500 would be needed simply to achieve the same annual rate of purchase. This would not require more processing staff, although the unit cost for that staff would also increase, resulting in a much higher unit cost per item added to the collections. Thus, while the library budget has increased substantially, its output has not changed. If, however, the institution is unable to maintain even the same amount of financial support for library materials, the whole picture will change dramatically. A series of choices must be made:

(1) The first choice must be not between types of purchases but as to what proportion of each will be reduced. It is impossible, in such a situation, to retain all subscriptions since left to thcmselves over a four-year period those same subscriptions would increase in cost to over $870,000 (Table 8), leaving next to nothing for any other expenditure (Diagram 5).

(2) A further choice is then required between areas of support, as to which shall be most curtailed. This is clearly a political choice, but one which must be guided by future projections. If those areas with the highest cost increase rates are left untouched, the effects on others will be that much the more drastic.

(3) Whatever choice is made concerning the materials to be acquired, there will be effects on the staff required for processing. Because of the differences in processing costs, reductions in serial subscriptions will have less impact on support costs than reductions in books. In either case, choices will have to be made as to vacant positions to be collapsed or transfers to be made.

(4) If the reduction is sufficiently great, alternative sources of information will almost certainly have to be found. A likely short-

Table 8. Changes in the Distribution of Expenditures on Library Materials.

	Base Year	2nd Year	3rd Year	4th Year	5th Year
"Books"	400,000	325,000	238,750	139,563	25,497
Periodicals	500,000	575,000	661,250	760,437	874,503
Binding	50,000	50,000	50,000	50,000	50,000
	$950,000	$950,000	$950,000	$950,000	$950,000

Diagram 5. Distribution Trends of Expenditures on Library Materials.
(Expressed in $000)

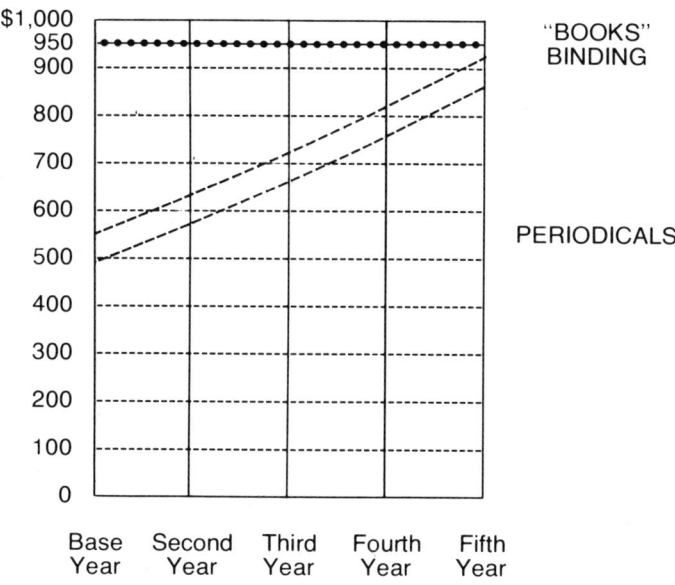

term trend would be a dramatic increase in interlibrary borrowing, or funds might be diverted to some cooperative scheme. In either case it is likely that staff support will have to be transferred to the units affected. The choice made of the alternative to be introduced will in turn depend on other factors both internal and external. Here the belated recognition that services cost money referred to earlier may play a decisive role in fund allocation. As increasing numbers of libraries charge for interlibrary lending and for photoduplication, it may prove desirable economically for the library to pay these costs rather than carry out multiple searches for a lending libary that does not charge, and desirable socially since any other course of action would restrict borrowing from another library to those who could afford it.

(5) The choice in all these areas may also have to be between short-term and long-term action. The decision will be influenced by the likely duration of the crisis, and by the maneuverability available to the library. A series of small adjustments may be less disrupting than one major one, but the latter may be the only way of meeting the institution's claims on the library.

This digression is intended principally to emphasize that whether decisions, large or small, are made or not, there will be considerable changes in the patterns of expenditure and investment. Ignoring them will not make such changes go away and may only make them worse.

CONSTRAINTS

The constraints that operate within a library may be classified as internal and external. While it might appear that internal constraints are the more easily dealt with, this is not necessarily the case. A building with no more room for the expansion of the collection is clearly a severe constraint. A possible solution, the occupation by shelves of reading or service areas, may be totally unacceptable because of the violence it does to other goals. Other similar situations will no doubt occur to the reader.

Internal constraints are those which arise from the nature and the limitations of the library itself. The nature of libraries is to provide resources, access to them and assistance in their use. Any action which tends to reduce the library's capacity to provide these services may be seen as unnatural and will result in staff and user dissatisfaction. One of the most obvious examples is the crowded stack which reduces access and frustrates one of the primary goals. Another is the difficulty of ensuring the instant ability to check out material. While the first would be amenable to a solution based on capital expenditure, that solution would take time and until it was completed the constraint itself would grow, requiring the application of one or more interim solutions. Another answer, unacceptable because it runs contrary to the entire philosophy of the library, would be to postpone the purchase of all but the most essential new materials. Quite apart from the controversy sure to result from the process of choosing the most essential purchases, this procedure would ensure that at some future time the library would have to repair the damage caused by this temporary suspension of a major goal. Nevertheless, recognition of such a constraint would be a very proper consideration in the allocation of funds. The problem of handling the circulation of materials arises from a common situation where activities are very unevenly distributed and it is uneconomic to structure an entire operation to deal with maximum flow. The same argument applies to any extension of hours. Unless the institution is prepared to subsidize the library's activities by paying for the necessary staff to provide services during hours when those services are required by relatively few members of the academic community, the library must choose to remain open at those times when greater numbers of users are present, even though it may be argued that the services provided to the few are more valuable per head.

The conversion from manual to automated activities presents another variety of internal constraint. From the adoption of an automated project, say of the circulation system, until its implementation may be a period of weeks, months or years, depending on its complexity. During that time the existing system must be maintained. Unless extra funding is available, both expenses must be met from the same financial resources. Further investment in the manual system does not seem justified and yet it must continue to function. It is likely therefore that files will be mended rather than replaced and that other equipment will be allowed to deteriorate, provided it does not hinder the process too greatly. Equally, investments in the new system can be made only as money is available and usually as late as possible, since it is undesirable to have equipment which is not being used, but on which maintenance and other charges must be paid. Such constraints are likely to be the most vexing of all, since they require constant attention and constant adjustment. Moreover since they are largely invisible (books stacked on the floor are only too visible) they tend to be overlooked by all those not directly involved, yet their priority may be the highest. The library administrator is therefore required to maintain this priority in the face of misunderstanding and even opposition.

Internal constraints provide problems that are partly amenable to internal solution, principally the reallocation of resources between uses. They must, however, remain partly unsolved for shorter or longer periods of time, because the solution is partly dependent on the resolution of other internal problems.

External constraints may be assigned to the institutional environment and to the national enviroment. Institutional constraints of an administrative nature are most frequently expressed in policies or instructions, relating either to academic or fiscal matters. They are least are expressed and therefore can be understood, interpreted and applied to library operations. They may be unwelcome—for example, a freeze on hiring; or they may provide longed-for support—for example, administrative approval of a policy enforcing faculty compliance with lending regulations. But their principal characteristics are their measurability and their universal applicability. Nonadministrative constraints may, however, be exceedingly difficult either to describe or to cope with. A very common problem relates to the apparent carelessness with which the faculty expands, constracts or modifies the academic program. Unless the library is given the opportunity (and the money) to respond quickly to such changes, disharmonies develop which are no one's fault but which create frictions that may alienate previously strong supporters of the library. Equally, on the day-to-day level, one faculty member may send his class to the library, without notice, to fulfil a rather complicated assignment. The library copes once, perhaps twice; but if the practice becomes widespread, other activities may collapse while the library tries to adjust to a new pattern of use. None of these concerns may seem insuperable, taken one at a time, but together they comprise the unpredictability of academia which is a major problem for libraries. It is no comfort to say that such aberrations are predictable on a statistical basis. The problem lies in their very specific location and timing. A secular shift in the methods of teaching and learning is self-evident when examined afterward. While it is happening it appears bewildering and largely meaningless.

For a library, however, the most significant external constraints are those over which neither library nor institution has any control. The greatest constraint of all, fluctuations in the willingness of society to fund higher education, is only too well-known; but is well outside the scope of this book. Inflation is the next most important factor.

All academic administrators are used to the effects of national inflation, although it has received much greater attention in recent years, when public funding has been more difficult to obtain. The problem is often to find correct measurements which can be used. A recent study published for the Department of Health Education and Welfare[2] provides a very useful survey of prices and indexes with which all librarians concerned with budgets should familiarize themselves. In addition, the various library material price indexes[3] clearly reveal the effect of price increases on the purchasing power of any library. Concepts such as that of an implicit price deflater, the comparison of purchasing power of current as against constant dollars, are useful in considering the implications of inflation, but are of limited use in discussion with those who are unsophisticated economically. Sometimes it is difficult to translate their effects into understandable terms. This is, in part, because these effects cannot easily be believed by most people, even when they themselves have stopped buying books or have resigned from learned societies because of the cost. They seem to think libraries are so large and buy so many books that one or two fewer, even one or two thousand fewer, cannot make much difference. The fact is, of course, that this nonpurchase or that one does not make a great deal of difference, but over the years the cumulative difference is very great indeed.

The demonstration of the effects of inflation on a book-buying program requires very skillful handling. It is easy to alarm people, who will on reflection ask for evidence of the academic effects of reduced acquisitions rates. On the other hand, it is easy to downplay the effects in order to avoid answering difficult questions on the use made of the collections. In such circumstances it is wise to begin with statements setting out the cost of staying put. No action at all will require that more money be spent in precommitted areas, notably serial subscriptions. As a result, if no effort is made to meet the costs of inflation all other kinds of expenditure will be lowered. Not only that, but, because unit prices will increase, there will be a compound reduction. If, in our sample budget, no further money were supplied for library materials, assuming price increase rates of 15 percent for periodical subscriptions and 10 percent for books, the distribution would change as in Table 8. This is admittedly a straight-line projection and presumes that no subscriptions are canceled. The point at issue, however, is that an apparent no-change decision has in fact set the scene for long-term farreaching changes of staggering magnitude. It is even more sobering to consider the quantities of units such an expenditure distribution represents. In the base year, assuming a unit cost of $10 per book and $20 per subscription, 45,000 books and 25,000 subscriptions were purchased. In the fifth year 25,000 subscriptions are still being purchased, but only 1,742 books.

From such a beginning it is relatively simple to construct a case for increased support in all but a general fiscal disaster. The real figures with which the individual librarian must work are far more complicated, because the distribution of expenditures differs with each library.[4] National trends do, however, supply a valuable standard against which to measure local activity, while the individual elements of the indexes are helpful in establishing the likely costs of a new program.

Diagram 6. Buying Power Expressed in Units Purchased, of a Static Budget for Library Materials.

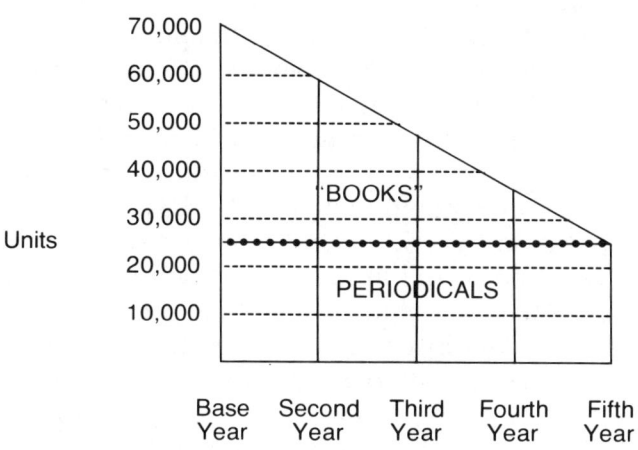

Note: Binding Costs Are Excluded.

Because expenditures on library materials constitute so high a proportion of a library's expenditure, other items are frequently overlooked. Such an omission is very dangerous. Given certain levels of activity, certain inescapable expenditures flow from them. Catalog cards, paper, IBM cards,—in fact, all paper products—are integral parts of a library's operations and are, by reason of their functions, seldom, if ever, reuseable. All of them, too, are subject to the same price increases as books and are even more necessary for library's continued fulfillment of its purposes. Nor is this the only factor. Equipment, once purchased, must be serviced. The most usual way to arrange for this is through the purchase of a maintenance contract. Although strictly speaking this is contract for service, it is more usually classified with other purchases of goods. While it may be possible to postpone or reduce service on typewriters, a maintenance contract for microform readers is essential while that for computer equipment must be regarded as an integral part of the operation. Telephone and postage costs are inseparably liked to the function of the library as a communication center.

All these items have in common one thing: their costs are externally determined. Any institution proposing to continue buying these goods and services has no option but to accept price increases. The only avenue for savings lies in decreased consumption, for the most part such decreases cannot be made. In that sense expenditures for goods and services represent the least flexible portion of a library's budget and consequently the one most likely to be affected by inflation. Because it is not possible to buy fewer such goods, more money will be spend in buying the same. Unless the extra money is provided to cover these price increases, the same activities can only be maintained at the expense of others.

PRIORITIES

In any budgetary action, the setting of priorities must itself have first priority. While it is true that, because it deals in gross relationships and results in an equation which provides the answer, formula budgeting removes some of the priority-setting from the librarian; but many special needs and programs must be taken into account by the librarian,[5] and, after the budget has been arrived at, its internal distribution is the responsibility of the library administrator. Decisions, then, must be made by the librarian concerning what must continue to be done.

It is unlikely that any librarian will decide consciously to close the library, or to discontinue issuing materials to borrowers. Equally, it is essential to maintain some order in the stacks, so that what the library owns can continue to be accessible. The margin of choice in these areas is not great. Of their nature, these services are simple and relatively easy to quantify, yet they are also basic to the continuing operation of the library. Any decision to continue or to modify them is susceptible to measurement and analysis and therefore readily transformable into a budget need. This does not mean that the decision would only be made to maintain or expand such services, but that the effects of changes in hours of opening or rules for borrowing can be measured. The identification of such basic areas is a primary step toward the isolation of areas more susceptible to scrutiny that can therefore contribute more to any reallocation of resources.

In making these choices two concepts should be kept in mind. The first is that of marginal efficiency of investment, which relates to the return received from the last unit of investment in a given product or process. How much, in other words, can be invested in a certain activity before the returns start to fall off? Discovering that point may be very difficult in an academic environment, but it tends to be evidenced by clumsiness of activity, system failures more or less serious in themselves and by the appearance of busy work, some of which arises simply from the need to hold the operation together. At such a point, alternatives must be sought, which may be organizational or mechanical in nature. The injection of extra funds seldom does more than compound the inefficiency.

The second concept is the need to consider the effectiveness of a library's services. Whether it relates to how well the library can handle its purchasing routines or whether it can indeed deliver that book when purchased into a user's hand, this is the political counterpart to the concept of efficiency. Effectiveness automatically introduces the user into the equation and requires that the library administrator consider "community rather than institutional costs and benefits" as part of the allocation process.[6] Unless this is done, it is not possible to arrive at true priorities for a service institution. It follows from this that trade-offs must also be considered. For example, in staffing a circulation desk, it may be necessary to decide that a two minute or even a five minute wait at peak periods is not incommensurate with good service, because the marginal investment required to ensure instant response at all times is so great that there is no way in which the institution could provide it. Thus in making any decision on priorities, it is also necessary to set limits and not pursue the "right objective . . . beyond some reasonable point."

Reference was made earlier to the necessary choices that are forced on an acquisitions program by budgetary troubles. These, however, represent but one side of the set of priority choices that must be made. Is it in the words of an earlier era to be "guns before butter"? What priority has the maintence of an acquisitions program? Lip service is often paid to the need for buying books, even while the power to buy is steadily being reduced. Admitted that many books bought by most libraries do not earn their keep, except in a secular sense, it is still true that lack of collection development according to a relatively steady pattern bears a close resemblance to the deferred maintenance which drastically reduced railroad performance in the U.S. in the early seventies. A decision is therefore required on the level and pattern of acquisitions to the maintained: level, because that will require a corresponding financial investment; and pattern, because that will determine the distribution of supporting costs. Interpretation and decision is greatly assisted by the statistics that have been collected, because they will reveal the differential staff needs of each pattern. The maintenance of existing subscriptions combined with reduced monograph acquisition is in work terms a totally different load from that resulting from reduced subscriptions and a maintained level of monograph acquisitions. Finally, the distribution pattern decided on will have further service impact, particularly in terms of shelving or stack maintenance, but also in terms of how effective the collection is in supplying the needs of users, with consequent effects on reference and bibliographic service staffs.

The many public services a library provides are not easily convertible into dollar expenditures; nor, even if that has been done, is it easy to determine which among them is most important or valuable or necessary. The difficulty lies in the use of words such as "desirable" or "necessary," which are, of course, susceptible of individual interpretation. If the words "efficient" and "effective" can be used, some of the difficulty vanishes. It is no doubt possible to run a very efficient library which buys books, catalogs them, shelves them and allows them to be borrowed. It is even conceivable that it could be effective within severely prescribed limits if every user knew exactly what he wanted. Given, however, the general context of American education, it is unlikely that such a library would demonstrate anything like a level of effectiveness commensurate with the needs and aims of the institution. In almost any situation, therefore, short of fiscal catastrophe, the maintenance of some kinds of public services are an essential part of the library's goals, regardless of the fact that neither the services themselves nor their effects can very readily be measured.

The justification of costs in public service areas has always been difficult. The library profession has made this even more difficult by the persistent use of the word "free," as if anything were free. What was meant, of course, was that access was free because no individual charge was levied. But, in fact, everyone contributed through taxes whether they wanted to use library services or not. The resulting income was apportioned as seemed right to the librarian between resources, processing and public service functions. For the most part this judgement was never questioned until the time came when the providers of public money had themselves to consider alternative uses. Asked the question why all the taxpayers should subsidize so special a function as libraries or higher education, librarians and administrators had only philosophical answers that were not enough to keep the cashbox full. Faced with this dilemma, more thoughtful librarians realized that it was necessary to measure costs and benefits and to use these measurements as a way of deciding what services to provide. Further prolongation of fiscal difficulty has forced many libraries to consider charging for the recovery of costs. These charges may vary from processing surcharges on overdue fines, to overhead recovery on data-base searching. The most striking decision however, is to charge for interlibrary loan services. All these actions demonstrate the use of fiscal policy to achieve two ends: (1) to reduce the demand from external sources, and (2) to recover costs incurred.

Even supposing that these actions have been taken only under pressure, they do indicate a willingness to place both a cost and a value on a service, which is a new thing for academic libraries. The same principles can and should be applied to all services to detemine how much the library can affort to invest in them. The natural desire to improve one's services (*i.e.,* answer more questions) may have to be restrained because other activities need the investment more. Paradoxically, it may be necessary to reduce the promotion of some services because the library is unable to support the resulting increased activity. As a final paradox it may be necessary to increase the library's investment in activities designed to produce self-directed library users in order to free other reference personnel to handle the more complex reference work they cannot presently cope with.

Explanatory statements on reference or similar staff needs are difficult to prepare principally because those who receive them for scrutiny are seldom familiar with or even aware of such services. It is unfortunate that no standards are available providing staff/user ratios or suggesting how much reference work may be anticipated from a certain community of users. Since standards can be a two-edged sword, their lack in this area is perhaps not altogether to be regretted.[7]

SYNTHESIS

It is important not to separate categories of expenditure in one's thinking. Such artificial divisions are necessary in setting up specific accounts, but library programs are supported by an amalgam of expenditures ranging all the way from administrative overhead down to daily expenditures for supplies. All these expenditures must be available or the programs will be unsuccessful. The variable effects of inflation on each category of expenditure, as well as the degree of essentiality of each, must be taken into account.

The budget request that is prepared as a result of the foregoing analysis will take its shape, of course, from the requirements and instructions of the institution. No single set of precepts can be given that will assist in this task. The most important thing is to remember to present facts and figures, and to be able to justify them if asked. The next most important thing is to present requests properly in accordance with the instructions, yet to know when to insist on an exception. For example, the instructions from the Office of Budget and Planning at the Pennsylvania State University set out quite clearly the budgetary priorities of the institution:

> Most members of the University community already are aware of the sober financial realities within which the University must do its budget planning for the current fiscal year and those immediately ahead.
> In this context, two ingredients are essential: (1) Limitation of allocations related to employment of additional continuing faculty or staff members to those instances which are *absolutely essential*; and (2) Strong emphasis on further "belt tightening" and internal rebudgeting *within* each Aministrative Division—without further resource allocations other than partial provisions for increased operating costs.
>
> . . .
>
> First priority . . . shall be given to:
>
> 1. TEACHING WORKLOAD . . . reflected in increases in credit hours, *where it is clearly demonstrated* that the Administrative Division . . . *as a whole* does not now have sufficient resources to absorb all or a part of the teaching work-load increase.
> 2. TEACHING SUPPLIES . . . based on *documented* serious deficiencies . . .
> 3. STUDENT WELFARE . . . nonacademic proposals with *documented* direct and essential relationships to the welfare of students.
> 4. PLANT OPERATIONS . . . based on documented unavoidable increases in operating expenses . . .

5. STAFF BENEFITS . . . based on *documented* unavoidable increases . . .

In the event that any funds are available for allocation after covering priority situations defined above, further allocation priorities may be determined for:

6. COST INCREASES . . . documented unavoidable substantial cost increases, such as postage rates . . . or prices of books and periodicals (in the case of University Libraries only) . . .

7. PRESENT DEFICIENCIES . . . documented serious deficiencies in current permanent budgets—where there is clear evidence that the sources of temporary supplements are no longer available . . .

8. NECESSARY SUPPORT . . . *necessary* increased service will be provided.

9. PLANNING IMPLEMENTATION . . . implement major recommendations in the University's Academic Policy Plan . . . unless such recommendations are found to be infeasible for financial or other reasons.[8]

Given the limitations that are placed on new program developments, it would be impossible to assign a high priority to new services, or even to the expansion of existing ones. Yet within the same guidelines, a strong case can be made for the support of reference instruction services based on the expected increase in enrollment, provided evidence is produced that internal redistribution of resources cannot meet the need. Here the careful analysis of existing expenditures in relation to the library's programs provides exactly the supporting documentation needed, since it enables the library administrator to pinpoint the necessary facts and to demonstrate the effects of change.

The budget request must convey clearly the priorities of the library and the financial support required to meet those priorities. It must do so with a minimum of additional documentation, and that documentation must align the priorities of the library with those of the institution. It must not disguise the effects of failure to meet the required level of financial support, but equally it must not overstate them. It is no good threatening to close the library, when such an action will not be allowed to take place. But if the dropping of certain services or acquisitions programs will be necessary, such reductions must be stated clearly and calmly.

In nearly all cases, even where the most elaborate formulae are used or where there are multitudes of separate funds and endowments, the resulting statements are succinct. It is difficult to make one column of figures look impressive, and the librarian charged with preparing the budget request frequently feels let down when all that work produces only two or three sheets of paper. Nevertheless, on those two or three sheets of paper—more correctly, on their proper preparation—depends the future of the library.

NOTES
1. Baumol and Marcus (1973), p. 40.
2. Halstead (1975).
3. Although it is assumed that most readers will be familiar with the indexes available it seems worthwhile to summarize them here. Indexes are presently maintained which cover U.S. book publishing in several categories, the most important of which, to libraries, is the U.S. Hardcover Trade Books Index. Vitally important indexes are those for U.S. Periodicals and U.S. Subscription Services. Others are being developed for microforms, newspapers and antiquarian materials; and further work is being carried out to develop better indexes for foreign publications.

Work on these indexes is under the general control and supervision of the Library Materials Price Index Committee, a committee of the Resources Section, of the Resources and Technical Services Division of the American Library Association. The indexes themselves are available in *The Bowker Library Annual,* which groups all available indexes together; *The Publishers Weekly,* where each February the book price indexes for the previous year are published; and *The Library Journal,* where in May or June the latest periodical price indexes are published.

In future, microform indexes will appear in *Microform Review.* All librarians should be familiar with these indexes and with the other, related information appearing in these publications.

4. The best way to use indexes is still a matter of debate. In his article, "The Validity of Book Price Indexes for Budgetary Projections," pp. 5–12, Axford argues strongly in favor of the development of local indexes. After mature consideration, the Library Materials Price Index Committee considered that some clarification was needed. The resulting "Book Price Indexes," pp. 97–98, states the use of national indexes as indicators of long-term trends.
5. Fairholm, pp. 332–333.
6. Raffel and Shishko (1969), p. 47.
7. Hirsch, p. 161.
8. Pennsylvania State University (1976), pp. 2–5.

Chapter 8

Presentation and Justification of a Budget Request

> *Decision-makers at different stages of the budget cycle operate from different decision-making perspectives and therefore require different configurations of budgetary information.*
> (Lyden, October 1975).

It is not likely that a circulation clerk, the head of reference, the director of the library, the president of the university and finally the budget secretary for the state or the state legislature will have the same view of a library budget, although they are all involved in it in different ways. To one it may affect the entire context of daily life while to another it is a remote portion of a part of the whole which must be considered. It is partly a matter of the expectations each has of the budget itself and partly a matter of how each one views the budget process. The objective in the presentation and justification of a budget request is to obtain from the audience both understanding of and agreement with the goals stated in the budget.

All budgets are premised on "certain activities—using certain resources, which result in some intended impact on society."[1] The perspective, however, makes a considerable difference to the amount, kind and ordering of information required and to the manner in which it is received. This is not an argument for the suppression of information but for the realization that information structured to meet one need may well be a hindrance to the understanding of a specific budget by another audience. While it is necessary to explain the various constraints and possibilities inherent in any budget, exhaustive discussion is likely to cloud thinking and dull perceptions. The administrator at a higher level is well aware of the many unpredictable factors that may distort and change a budget either in the course of the approval process or during the time of its implementation, but to dwell on these is to reinforce the view that no one expects adherence to any rules or limitations. Equally, of course, to insist too strongly on known limitations or likely constraints is to suggest in advance that no attempt will be made to overcome or modify the effects of such limitations. Steering a course between these extremes requires all the skill available to any administrator.

The presentation should answer three questions:

(1) What activities are to be carried out?
(2) What resources are required to carry out these activities?
(3) What will the results be and how will they be measured?

Naturally each question comprehends within itself a wide range of subquestions, and implicit in each one are why and how much.

As stated by Morris Gelfand, "the budget is conceived of as a planning and control document and an important vehicle of communication and persuasion."[2] If it is to achieve the last stated goals, it must do more than state certain facts—it must convince the reader that they are desirable and attainable. It is necessary, also, to be aware of the fact that the budget presented will, as it passes further on, lose its identity. Gelfand properly stresses that "before undertaking the preparation of a budget, it is essential to identify priorities in the light of what is known about the needs, interests and nature of the community."[3]

The goals and objectives stated in the budget and its accompanying documentation must therefore be in harmony with the goals of those greater units. This harmony is not a superficial one, such as may arise from not rocking the boat by making outrageous demands, but from a clear demonstration that the requirements stated in the library budget support and reinforce the goals of the institution.[4]

The answers provided to the three basic questions should take into account institutional as well as library needs. For example, the need to maintain an acquisitions program is not self-justificatory. The legislator who asks why any more books are needed is the exception. The more probing question, why this many and not that many, is much more difficult to answer and cannot be brushed aside. Support may be sought from the budgets of comparable institutions, by reference to formulae such as that of Clapp and Jordan,[5] but the most effective support will be figures showing actual use and information demonstrating the relationship of the acquired materials to the educational program of the university. This is the kind of performance standard referred to by Axford,[6] and is important in combating the ignorance, even suspicion, commonly expressed in the attitude of administrators toward libraries.

The difficulty experienced by librarians in presenting their case is, however, shared by the institution's own administrators. As Summers puts it:

> Budget analysts seem more at home with the governmental functions of law enforcement, regulation and licensing, than with less tangible programs relating to education and libraries.[7]

Library programs are eminently difficult to place a value on; and, though librarians seldom admit it, they are also eminently absurd when described in detail, which increases the difficulty in achieving both understanding and appreciation of the need for those programs. The author remembers presenting a detailed defense of a request for increased cataloging support and watching amazement and disbelief vie for supremacy in the face of the most senior administrator present. It may have been his kind heart rather than his head that persuaded him to endorse the request, but it was more likely to have been the agreement of the analysts whose investigations made it clear that it was not a phony request.

Activities should be stated both in library terms and in terms relating to the activities of the institution. This matching of intent is assisted by using the terms in which the original budget instructions were couched. Adherence to those instructions, and use wherever possible of the terms used there, will improve the acceptability of the presentation.

It is desirable to be able to demonstrate what is within the library's control and what is not, and to highlight the limited range of choices actually available as distinct from the pseudochoices frequently offered. Most libraries are severely limited in the choice of alternatives by the expectations of their user community. Since the administrators reviewing the library's budget request represent that community, the range of choice available is even more severely limited than if the reviewer were simply concerned with the fiscal consequences of choice.

Basic services such as the lending of materials cannot be abandoned without abandoning one of the main goals of the library. Once this decision has been made, certain others inevitably follow. In the fulfilment of this primary goal the library has to undertake certain kinds of activities, ranging from the actual circulation of books through reshelving to measures designed to protect the collections and reduce loss or theft in the interests of the larger community. These activities are controlled in kind by the systems adopted by the library. The systems may be modified or new ones substituted, but this is essentially within the library's power to decide. Quantitative control on the other hand, other than the most elementary limitations imposed by controlling the hours of opening, rests with the users. Since it may be presumed that these users, by coming to the library, consulting and borrowing books, are fulfilling some portion of the goals of the college, the library is bound to respond in as generous a way as possible. If this is so, then limitations contrary to such a goal are unacceptable. Decisions relating to the marginal utility of extra hours of opening may be made, but arbitrary limits on the amount of material that may be borrowed must be rejected in the interests of library users. The library is therefore bound to provide the necessary resources to meet this goal, even if it means diminishing the resources provided to meet other goals. This condition is a primary example of the external control to which library programs are subject.

Other limitations are practical rather than political. A good example of this is the size of the library materials budget. There is no limit to the number of books that could be bought if the money were available. The desirable number of book purchases is decidedly less than the total number that could be made if money were unlimited, but probably more than there is likely to be money for. It is also controlled by what other resources are likely to be available for purchasing, processing and storing them. It is therefore impractical to ask for more than can profitably be spent. And since a request for a large increase would focus attention on a program which appears out of line, care must be taken to demonstrate that any such request is realistic and serves the interests of the institution. The essential thing is to demonstrate that the amounts requested are not arbitrarily chosen.

Libraries, too, have little choice in whether or not they are to provide reference and information services. If they did not, a primary reason for their existence would vanish and a warehouse or storehouse could be substituted. The range, style and variety of services can, however, be controlled, even if only to a limited extend. This may be a matter of necessity (*e.g.*, lack of staff) or a policy (*e.g.*, not providing bibliographic help which students should perform for themselves, or insisting that certain procedures be carried out by the user before calling on the library for further service). Other kinds of limitations arise from the numbers of users and the intensity of use. It is, for example, less necessary for special collections to be accessible on a round-the-clock basis than it is for reserve books just before an examination period. For all these situations it is possible to discuss alternative service patterns and to develop, however crudely, some cost-benefit or unit-cost information which can aid in the making of rational choices. This information can then be used as evidence to support the choices made and demonstrate that they were made on some rational basis. Such a presentation makes it possible for those evaluating a budget proposal to choose between alternatives according to the values adopted by the institution.

Finally, there are those matters which, while marginal, may not be amenable to being turned on and off at will. A library may have adopted reclassification as a goal, yet the actual production each year can be varied. Nevertheless, if at the end of a year a particular project is half completed (say the holdings of a branch library), it is impossible simply to stop without serious and undesirable consequences. The project must therefore be completed even if after that the energies of the team involved must be turned elsewhere temporarily.

In all this the goal has been to demonstrate what is planned to be done with the money allocated. The documentation must be carefully prepared.

> Statements which merely prove that a program is desirable do not fulfill the needs of a superior who is faced with the necessity of reducing the total amount requested by the subordinates, not because he thinks the requests are for undesirable or unnecessary purposes, but simply because the pattern is too big for the cloth.[8]

Any statements must therefore show what will be done, how it relates to existing or proposed programs and what will be the result of any increase or decrease. The amount of detail provided must be tempered by the audience to which it is to be presented. The chancellor or provost is more likely to want information about the improved quality of service that is planned. A budget analyst, on the other hand, will follow up in detail such matters as the trends shown in activity indicators, if such are used, or question apparent contradictions between verbal and financial versions of the same program.

It is unlikely that the entire budget will have to be defended at any one hearing. It is much more likely that deviations from the current state will be questioned. The information sought is why the change has been proposed and what effect it will have. To be persuasive, the answers must show that it is not arbitrary and that it flows naturally from the goals of the library. The administrator will, in turn, have to decide whether the institution can afford to support the change or not; and consequently, the library administrator must be prepared to suggest alternative ways of doing the same thing (more cheaply) or to postpone or abandon the proposal, while still maintaining the viability of the library program as a whole. He must therefore be able to say clearly what the library can or will do if the answer is negative.

The extreme case occurs when the library administrator must respond to a hold-the-line or a reduced budget. Responding to such proposals requires the analytical knowledge developed through one of the program budget styles. Budgets which provide anything less than increases to match inflation require reexamination of the whole budget. The greater the discrepancy, the more thorough the reexamination and the restructuring that must be carried out. In such a presentation it is essential to demonstrate why certain choices were made and not others and what their institutional effects would be. A problem that is frequently encountered relates to the perceptions of the library held by nonlibrarians. As Peter Drucker puts it:

> You start out with a very clear concept of what the library is, and the only thing is that none of your publics can possibly share that vision. It's an inside vision . . . the library to you is an end, but to your publics it is a tool. . . .[9]

Although the tone is slightly flippant, the perception is acute; and the later discussion of the budget and its justification[10] defines the problem very neatly in terms of the high cost of information. Effective use requires trained users or, in their absence, highly trained staff; but most outsiders still think in terms of cheap or free information which is easy to find. Overcoming this gap in perception is part of the purpose of budget presentations.

The use of statistics, such as circulation figures, or reference questions answered, contributes in part to narrowing the gap and, until we know better how to measure user satisfaction, they are the only figures most librarians have. They do, however, require careful use since it is very easy to fall into the trap of perpetual progression. For example, if for several years, the main reliance has been on increasing circulation figures, in a year when they do not increase, the principal rationale for increased support may be removed at a stroke. Amount of use, to be meaningful, must be related to the kinds and numbers of users. It is also necessary to distinguish between different kinds of use, whether in-house or by borrowing, or even by photocopying. In this way a composite picture can be drawn which is less easily distorted by the change of one component among many. These statistics are, in effect, being offered in answer to the question "How will the results be measured?" It is critical that the answer be in terms congenial to the library. There is, unfortunately, a lack of use standards, as distinct from standards of size. The latter sort of standard[11] can be useful as a referent, particularly when it can be shown that the library budget deviates considerably from that of similar institutions. Statistical tables published by the Association of Research Libraries and the Office of Education, Bureau of Libraries are useful in this respect. At most, however, the information currently available can give only a very general picture of present practices. Measurement of results by comparison with other libraries is neither easy nor satisfactory, but some such exercise is frequently required. It should be approached with caution and some stress placed upon its limitations. The difficulties arising from interinstitutional comparisons are discussed by Allen[12] in relation to the effects of formula budgeting. They are equally true of any comparison since no two institutions are truly alike. Moreover, since standards have generally been derived from practice it becomes extremely difficult to explain satisfactorily the reasons for deviations between one's own institution and the others being used as comparisons. To the extent that such extended consideration takes away from the simplicity of the presentation, it should be miminized, particularly since, in all likelihood, it will not be used in the further stages of budget consideration.

In the case of formula budgets it is, however, essential to emphasize special programs or responsibilities which require separate or incremental consideration. An example of the former might be a unique collection either supporting a unique educational program, or of regional or national importance, whose maintenance is essential to the goals of the institution. The latter kind of exception frequently applies to an interlibrary loan program where the lending is out of proportion to the borrowing. This may result from a regional or state plan or from the excellence of the library's collections. In the first instance it is proper to point out that services required of a library, over and above those deriving from its institutional role, are the proper object of subsidy. The library which by its eminence attracts the attention of other borrowers but which is not included within, say, a state plan is in a much more difficult position. If it is impossible to persuade the authorities ultimately responsible for the budget that such public services are beneficial to the institution and should be supported, it may be necessary to impose charges in order to retrieve some or all of the costs of the operation. A common difficulty with all such exceptions is the identification of actual costs, since inevitably they intertwine with those of other ongoing activities. The effort should, however, be made.

By way of summary, brief consideration can be given to what might be done for our model library with a suggested budget increase of 5 percent. The amount of new money available would be $160,000. The institution has begun a new graduate program which represents a new library field. The indicators show that the greatest pressures are in basic public services—circulation and reserves. The most significant external factor is inflation. Alongside these "facts" is a parallel set of desires, or—as usually expressed—"needs," which include faculty pressure for extra staff for special programs, librarian pressure for another cataloger and student pressure for longer hours.

Examination of the existing budget shows that to maintain the present library materials program will cost an additional $95,000, while basic cost increases in supplies amount to $5,000. Workload increases in circulation and reserves resulting from increased student enrollment will require about $25,000, to maintain the present staff work ratio, without extended hours. Following principles enunciated earlier, the new program will cost $30,500. The balance of the 5 percent ($4,500) will reduce but not eliminate the effect of inflation in other areas. Implicit in these figures are decisions to cope with acquisitions and cataloging needs by the redirection of savings into wages for those areas and to hold back on purchases other than basic supplies.

The net result is to expand acquisitions only by the minimal numbers required for the new program and to hold all other programs to approximately the same level. The most critical staff pressure-points have been eased, but possibly at the expense of later difficulties in technical processing. It has not been possible to respond to other faculty and student requests.

These are the facts to present to those responsible for reviewing the budget request. Other configurations might have been possible. For example, hours of opening could have been increased, but the cost of each hour extra per day was calculated to be $10,000 a year for minimal service and in addition the scheduling and regulatory problems would require adjustment of full-time schedules, the appointment of two more full-time personnel and realignment of wage expenditures for six departments. Weighed against the benefit derived by at most thirty to fifty users each day, the change appeared to be unwarranted when other needs were more pressing

Table 9. The State University Libraries.
Summary of the Budget Increase Requests for the Fiscal Year 197–

TOTAL AMOUNT	PERSONNEL	DISTRIBUTION LIBRARY MATERIALS	OTHER	UNIVERSITY PRIORITY
104,500	—	95,000	9,500	Inflationary costs. Required to maintain present program.
25,000	25,000	—	—	Maintenance of effort. Required to maintain staff/workload ratios.
30,500	15,000	15,500	—	Program development. Required to support new graduate program.
$160,000	$40,000	$110,500	$9,500	

during existing working hours. Reports on this alternative and any others considered may be used to support the library's priority decisions as being in line with real needs and the institution's priorities. Condensed, the request would then be as shown in Table 9.

Details would, of course, be provided both in accompanying documentation and in any oral or written presentation. Succinct as it is, however, this statement indicates what is being asked for, where it will be placed in the budget, why it is needed and how it relates to university and to library priorities.

NOTES
 1. Lyden (October, 1975).
 2. Gelfand, p. 500.
 3. *Ibid.*, p. 496.
 4. Natchez and Bupp, pp. 951–963. In this article the authors present an instructive analysis of governmental budget-making which illustrates the difficulties inherent in relating to one another the many separate decisions made during the budgetary process.
 5. Clapp and Jordan, pp. 371–380.
 6. Association of Research Libraries, (1975), p. 1179.
 7. Summers, p. 1179.
 8. Lyden and Miller (1965), p. 130.
 9. Drucker, p. 5.
 10. *Ibid*, p. 13.
 11. "Standards for College Libraries" (October, 1975). Standard 8, which is concerned with budgets, offers only generalities; but other standards, concerned with objectives, collections and services, suggest a framework for making comparisons with other institutions.
 12. Allen (1972), Appendix A, p. 32.

Chapter 9

Setting up the Budget

The allocation of a fixed budget represents a set of decisions about which functions should be fulfilled, and thus which objectives should be met and which users should be satisfied at the relative expense of other objectives and users. (Raffel and Shisko, 1969.)

In the best of all possible worlds the administrator faced with setting up a budget for the next year would have enough money to meet all known and probable needs. Moreover, the exact amount of money available would be known well in advance. Usually neither of these desirable situations exists. Most frequently the administrator is required to allocate a budget which will not meet all demands and which may well contain a considerable portion of possible or estimated funds. Even when exact budget amounts are known, there may have been changes in unit costs or shifts in programs which were not allowed for when the budget was originally established. Not all institutions approach budget-making in the same way. In some cases, even individual positions are specified and may not be shifted around. In others, a formula may require a particular distribution, or may inhibit certain kinds of changes. The range will be from those which are control-oriented, where the emphasis is on detailed budget allocations and accountability, to those which are program oriented and the emphasis is on the desired results leaving the allocations relatively free, measuring achievement rather than the accounts which record those achievements.[1]

It is at this point in the process that the constraints imposed by the institutional budgetary approach manifest themselves. Whereas a line or object budget will be very specific and may also be very restrictive, it can offer a fair range for initiative if any movement is allowed between categories. It is also the kind of analytical arrangement that is required when finally setting up the accounts for the year. If these accounts must also be set up by program or department, there is a further reduction in flexibility. The situation becomes particularly critical when there have been program changes or shifts in social emphasis as shown by changes in enrollment or in the distribution of faculty, yet the shape of the budget is rigidly controlled and therefore unable to respond to change.

Similar kinds of problems derive from formula budgets, where the initial request is subjected to political influences and the end result may bear only superficial relationship to the original input.[2] Despite the appearance of objectivity in the formula approach, the final distribution of funds, even supposing all that was asked for is received, requires a good deal of care and involves subjective and intuitive factors. When political decisions elsewhere have interfered with the "pure" request, the distribution may become very difficult indeed, if the attempt is made to marshal resources to achieve the goals represented by the original budget request.

Program budgets present the greatest flexibility, but this is often so only in appearance, because most activities will continue as before and there are frequently external influences (such as tenure, union or federal rules and the inertial force of serial subscriptions) which may delay or inhibit any planned changes. The assumption of a zero-base budget each year and the recognition that changes are both necessary and desirable during the year, do, however, help the administrator in coping with change.

The level at which changes must be approved and the way in which approval is sought will also affect the setting-up of a budget. This, together with the cautions expressed above, should be borne in mind when considering the procedures and examples used in this chapter. The style of management used will also have its effect. Object-of-expenditure budgets tend to accompany an authoritarian style. PPBS budgets tend to require wide involvement and democratic style. All are, however, affected by the needs of the institution to respond to audit examination, in which the object is to discover whether the institution has in fact spent its money in accordance with the intent of the budget. The procedure will be to examine each of the three major areas of expenditure, to highlight problems and necessities and to suggest ways in which libraries can utilize money most effectively within their individual administrative constraints.

Although this arrangement by category of expenditure is chosen to simplify presentation, it must be remembered that programs comprehend expenditures from all categories. For example, there must be a relationship between the amount to be spent for library materials and the amount to be spent for processing staff. If that relationship is not maintained, backlogs may build up and service deteriorate. Adjustments within the budget should be directed toward maintaining a distribution appropriate to the array of tasks at hand.

PERSONNEL-RELATED EXPENSES

No matter what the budgetary process used, one of the end-products will be an allocation of a part of the budget to personnel. With any luck the distribution will not be rigidly specified. The assumption here will be that there is some degree of latitude in the assignment or reassignment of personnel. As with other categories, the present distribution will play a major role in determining the future. This is so mostly for nonbudgetary reasons; but, after all, federal or state regulations, or union rules on clerical grades, for example, are equally as meaningful as budget figures on paper.

The objective of any personnel budget distribution is "to attune the level of staffing to the work load."[3] There are no clear standards prescribing work loads. Rule-of-thumb estimates exist for many activities, or suggested ratios, but they must be recognized as general statements only, to be modified according to local need and circumstance. Some of the formulae presently employed use performance standards of a sort to arrive at gross figures.[4] The standard-times approach is described by Fairholm,[5] who reminds us that "library staffing presents problems of rationalization and equality" and requires some "common ground" for decision-making. Forecasting techniques[6] are helpful, but our present knowledge is not sufficient to employ these techniques at the departmental or unit level. Studies of this kind should be familiar to administrators who should be able to use the general principles as a guide for specific actions.

At whatever time the budget for the forthcoming year is established, there will usually be some vacant positions. In addition, the records for the current year will indicate the level of expenditure in such variable areas as wages or part-time appointments. These factors, together with advice on new positions allowed—or conversely, reductions in positions—can be used to assess the degree of flexibility available. It must, however, be remembered that in setting up new positions, or even in transferring them from one department to another, the salary or hourly rate may have to be adjusted. In institutions where some kind of position control program is in force, the necessary procedures for that will also have to be followed.

The indicators or forecasts or departmental reports will have indicated areas where increased support is required or where reductions can be entertained without significant changes in output or work load ratios. For example, fewer books may be purchased because of lack of funds, and parallel staff savings may be possible; but if it is likely that further money for acquisitions will be available later, any personnel savings may only be temporary. A further complication may be introduced where the existing vacancies do not match program areas where reduced activity is envisaged. In such instances any realignment may have to await later vacancies, or some adminstrative transfer procedure may have to be invoked.

Several other factors may be imposed on any situation. Because federal legislation sets minimum hourly rates, legislative action may change budgetary requirements overnight. Occasionally, the institution may have available or receive supplementary funds to cover such increases but most frequently they must be met from within existing budgets. The effect of such a requirement is to reduce the number of hours available. Similar problems attend the implementation of federal legislation relating to unemployment compensation. Again, individual units may be required to absorb such costs. The way in which this can be done and the ability of the library to do so without serious stress will be determined by the degree of flexibility allowed. Special conditions may govern the timing for filling vacant positions. These may restrict or deny any overlap for purposes of training, may even require a lapse of time before the new appointment, or, in extreme cases, a position freeze may require individual rejustification for all vacancies. In all such cases, the results will differ according to the disposition of monies saved during the continuing vacancy.

Clearly then in practice the establishment of a staff distribution will differ significantly from an ideal distribution. The object of any adjustments made in setting up a budget should be to move nearer to that ideal distribution. Vacant positions should be audited and the decision made to retain, transfer, abolish or modify each position. To illustrate the effects of a seemingly simple modification, let us see what may happen when a senior librarian position is vacant and is not to be retained in the same role. The present salary for a bibliographer position is $18,000. The exincumbent was of associate rank and had several years' experience. Even if a new appointment were made to the same position, a new incumbent with, say, fewer years of experience would be unlikely to receive the same salary, and might be offered a salary of $14,000. The $4,000 balance could be regarded as savings for use in bolstering another salary in a position likely to come vacant later, or it might be available for expenditure on wages. If this adjustment is made at zero-budget time, such a transfer can usually be made without loss to the library. Under some systems of budgetary control, however, the same adjustment made during the year may result in confiscation of the $4,000 difference to a central fund on which the library may or may not be able to draw. In other cases, the reverse is true. Whatever the situation, the officer preparing the budget must be aware of such consequences. Transactions involving the transfer or modification of several positions at the same time are correspondingly more complicated, particularly if they include the transfer of positions between categories of employee, say from professional to clerical.

In establishing any new positions, attention must be paid to equitability of salary. Most institutions plan for salary increases to become effective with the new fiscal year. Such adjustments may or may not be part of the base budget operations, but it is necessary to provide for each new or adjusted position a salary which is in line with prospective salaries for similar positions in the next year. Where there are scales or ranges of salary this is a relatively simple matter, since the instructions for establishing positions will usually specify at what point within a scale the new salary should be set. Where no such ranges exist, the best that can be done is to provide a salary similar to those paid to comparable employees.

By and large, however, the numbers of changes likely to be made in full-time positions will be few. The same need not be true of the distribution of part-time or wage employment. When contemplating change, the pattern of expenditure for the current year and activity changes indicated by statistics should be examined for congruence and adjustments made to reduce disparities. Care needs to be taken, however, to distinguish between cases in which departmental expenditures have exceeded budget as it were on principle rather than because of essential activity, and those where necessary activities have grown and should continue to be supported. Similarly, decreases in activity should be examined to determine whether the change is temporary or permanent.

What can be done by way of a wage budget depends largely on the controls exercised by the institution, together, of course, with state and federal regulations. In some situations, wages may be used only to employ students. In others, they may be applied to the whole range from professional librarian to high-school student. It is possible to depend too much on part-time help and it should never become the whole source of a department's staff, because, for the most part, there is no long-term commitment. Yet precisely because it is part-time, variable and generally not as subject to regulation as full-time employment, the help received from wage-payroll employees can play a significant part in a library's programs.

In establishing a wage budget for the year, careful attention should be paid to possible sources of funds. Frequently institutions permit savings from vacant positions to be rechanneled to wages. This has the beauty of retaining the expenditure within the personnel-related category. Such a practice requires that vacancies for the year be forecast and the amount of savings calculated in order to establish what proportion of the operating budget can be derived from that source. Because the future is not readily predictable in detail, any such allocation of funds should be on the conservative side. Moreover, one must be prepared for changes in institutional policy, particularly such extreme actions as position freezes or amercements—*i.e.,* a 2 percent levy on all budgets or the confiscation of last-quarter savings. Nevertheless, it is a sound policy to establish at budget-setting time the proportion of wage expenditure that can be expected from savings. Any extra will then be a bonus. The proportion of savings to regular budget should never be so high that loss of savings would cripple the program.

Recent years have seen several federal or state programs aimed either at direct student assistance or the relief of unemployment. Funds provided for such purposes do not usually show up in the library's budget. If they do, of course they must be handled as any other account. If they are handled centrally, their impact must be assessed when distributing the library's own funds. Some programs are limited either in object or in funding, some must be for special purposes, other must not replace existing employed persons. For such reasons most labor under the work-study program will be for routine tasks not requiring extensive training and will therefore have more impact on circulation, stack maintenance, and routine technical operations than on the more sophisticated reference, selection and cataloging functions. It is important not to work federal funds, which are subject to all the usual political hazards, into the portions of the budget which sustain the main activities of the library.

One further consideration regarding salaries must be borne in mind. It is usual for institutions to handle such matters as fringe benefits and similar overhead costs on an institution-wide basis. These fringe benefits include retirement payments, social security, hospitalization, and any other plan where both employer and employee contribute to the costs. The resulting expenditures may be prorated in calculating the operating costs of each unit, but the charges themselves are not distributed. If, however, certain positions are not paid from general funds, the originating unit may be required to pay for any or all fringe benefits. This method of accounting is almost always adopted for grant money, for nominated funds whatever the source. The calculation of such overheads is an important factor in grant applications. In certain circumstances even general administrative overheads are charged to the individual budget. The provision of money for these costs is particularly important in the case of, say, an endowed position, since it is very possible that in addition to the endowment income the library may have to find supplemental money. A different but parallel situation occurs when positions are paid jointly from two or more funds. The proportion chargeable to each fund may be predetermined, but may on the other hand be the subject of negotiation annually. When the division is calculated in terms of academic work load (*e.g.*, eight courses per year equals one full-time position) or in terms of months, and when salaries must be divisible by twelve, negotiation may be necessary over what are really infinitesimal sums. Neverless, if these details are not attended to, it is possible that over a period of years the proportions may change substantially. Finally, in this category of salary adjustment, the graduate assistantship may be considered. Here it is necessary to determine where other support payments, such as tuition, must be located in the budget. For example, if a library has ten terms of such assistantships, but the money for tuition payments has been provided in a separate budget, action that reduced the number of assistantships would reduce the tuition budget automatically; but if the assistantship were to be reestablished, the library would have to transfer the appropriate sum from its own budget to the tuition fund.

Although the preceding statements are most appropriate to an expanding budget, they apply whatever the situation. If, however, a budget is to remain static or to be reduced, a further set of considerations must come into action. What activities should be reduced? What can be reduced and what cannot? A budget reduction may be accompaned by the exhortation to "cut out the fat," or to increase productivity. The problem lies, of course, in identifying the fat; and for libraries which came late to the budget feast of the sixties, the fat may not be too noticeable. Most activities are not easily controlled by libraries. Almost the only one over which direct financial control can be exercised is the acquisition and cataloging of books, and here libraries face the fact that the collecting of books is one of their primary goals. If the cut is major, then of course acquisitions must take its share. In any lesser circumstance, the justifiable tendency is to avoid cuts in this area or at least to hold them to a minimum. Desirable but nonessential programs may be pruned or discontinued instead, though here the political repercussions—say, of discontinuing a faculty book delivery system—may outweigh the financial advantages. Controllable programs such as reclassification may be halted and hours of opening may be altered to reduce the amount of wages required. In all cases the intention should be to maintain basic services and to minimize distortions in the shape of the library program, since large flunctuations in critical areas may have long-term repercussions.

LIBRARY MATERIALS

More has been written about the allocation of the book buget than about almost any other library activity. In fact so intense has been the interest that almost all other budget areas appear neglected by comparison. In the light of this extensive literature, no attempt will be made here to cover more than basic points. One of the most recent contributions, by Marchant,[7] discusses the very interesting point that predicators, particularly in the area of acquisitions, have become increasingly less easy to use, signifying decreasing control over variables. This should come as no surprise to those who handle erratic budgets, but it obviously makes the application of various formulae much more difficult.

Discussions of the ideal size of book budgets and the most desirable distributions frequently lose sight of two important constraints. The first is where the library is now; and the second is that the ideal may not correspond with the reality, whether the latter is academic, political or pragmatic. Schad, in a very informative discussion of how allocation formulae arose, remarks that it has been the "almost uniform practice to base allocations on some form of historical data."[8] While such a practice is sometimes inhibitory, unless past practice has been persistently out of line with a reasonable distribution some credit must be given to the evident interest and spending ability of the affected areas. Schad is, however, reminding librarians of a very valid criticism of any untested theory when he says, "identified or projected needs are the only valid basis on which to base budgetary decisions" and "allocations should be the result of academic and fiscal planning that expresses identified needs in terms of dollars costs."[9]

The process of arriving at this goal is much more complicated than simply stating it. There has been much dispute over what factors are important and what statistical method should be used in arriving at a distribution. The commonest factors used have been numbers of students, numbers of programs (or courses), numbers of faculty and the like—frequently calling into use elaborate weighting mechanisms. Few of these proposals have been statistically validated, because most utilization factors are subjective and almost impossible to measure. Some progress has been made, particularly by McGrath, who has adopted an empirical model, based principally on circulation and price, both criteria being more or less adequately measurable.[10] It is the author's view that this approach can be be valuable adjunct activity, but not the sole basis of fund distribution, partly because it requires extremely sophisticated application that in effect destroys its simplicity, but mostly because, like almost all formulae, it ignores the effect of serial subscriptions, both their continuing existence and their differential inflation rates, and the ways in which one might measure their use.

Budgets for library materials must, in some degree, reflect the academic structure of the institution. Standards, particularly those used by accrediting agencies, tend to use numbers of students as a major (or indeed the only) criterion. Massman and Patterson state correctly that:

> An academic library's holdings can be determined only by the quantity and range of the materials being published which are relevant to the academic programs it is supporting, not by the traditional number-of-students criterion.[11]

Their article refers to a basic current buying program, but the same is true of older materials. Institutional administrators (and legislatures) are particularly prone to this error, because so much else of the institution's expenditure is conditioned by the number of students. The most recent *Standards for College Libraries* avoids this pitfall, but remnants of the mode of thought remain embedded in the text:

> A collection may be said to have quality for its purpose only to the degree that it possesses a portion of the bibliography of each discipline taught, *appropriate in quantity both to the level at which each is taught and to the number of students and faculty who use it.*[12]

A modified version of the Clapp-Jordan formula is used for arriving at basic collection size and, as usual, experience is quoted as hallowing a 5 percent annual growth rate. While all these considerations may be perfectly proper as part of a whole, they cannot substitute for sensitivity to the goals and needs of the institution. Although these goals will differ widely, Dix manages to combine neatly both quantitative and qualitative criteria:

> University library costs are related much less directly to numbers of students than they are to factors such as the number of fields offered, the nature of each field, the quality of the collections, and above all the research element.[13]

With these admonitions in mind and accepting the judgement of McGrath and his coauthors of their own work,

As with any statistical device, its use is to assist in a management decision. The statistics themselves cannot make this decision,[14]

an attempt can be made to determine which factors are relevant to the library and what its needs are at that particular time. No planning is forever; both the needs and the capacity to meet those needs will change. This year's distribution need not reveal uniform relationships to last year's, provided that the changes are justified by need and not the result of caprice.

It is perhaps useful first to distinguish between two kinds of need, basic and augmentational.[15] Basic needs can be seen as covering the minimal acquisitions required to keep the collections alive and responsive. They will relate almost exclusively to current output and will include all formats, both unitary and periodical. It may, of course, happen that there is not sufficient money to meet this need. Unless more money is forthcoming, the librarian will be forced to choose between areas; and in such an instance, patron use may very well be the critical measurement. Augmentation is a process concerned with additions aimed at quality, at strengthening that which is and with incremental programs which respond to changes and improvements in the institution and may also be designed to compensate for great differentials in costs between areas.

Factors to be considered may be grouped under two broad headings, institution-related and library-related. The institutional factors refer to the willingness of the institution (and society) to invest in given educational programs. This investment is represented by the number of faculty, the research being undertaken (if any), the extent and range of the courses offered, the number of credit-hours, the number of majors and the number of graduate students. It must be admitted at once that some of these statistics may represent either residual investment, as in the case of tenured faculty in a discipline where enrollment has dropped, or substitutional investments such as in a department which carries a very heavy remedial load or provides basic low-level service courses. In most institutions some system of weighting is used to represent the more costly upper division and graduate courses.[16] This might prove useful for the library, and would have the advantage of uniformity; but like most measures, it would be artificial to apply it across the board. Graduate work in the humanities, for example, is much more library-oriented, than, say, in physics, where a major part of the institutional investment consists of laboratories and equipment. This kind of weighting is implicit in most standards, particularly those developed from the Clapp-Jordan formula. Care has to be taken to minimize the overlap between academic disciplines. For example, the list of fields cited in the *Standards for College Libraries*[17] could easily result in unrealistic total budgetary demands and a quite unrealistic distribution of money. Nevertheless, as a first step towards a distribution, the setting up of an academic profile is essential.

Intermediate between institutional and library factors is program response to identified need. As suggested by Schad, one of the goals of any allocation should be to provide funds for the purchase of materials to augment the collections as and where indicated by a proper examination of those collections, both bibliographically and in relation to the educational and research programs of the institution. No formula can readily accommodate this need, since it is variable both in amount and in area of assignment.

A familiar example is the new program, so frequently started without any consideration of library needs. As suggested by Frank Barnes, "the librarian may well need to be less sympathetic and cooperative than he is at present. It is pointless for example to establish a new department . . . without providing additional funds for the library." His strictures on one-time grants and long-term requirements are fully justified. "Earmarked grants have the merit of short-term financial plenty but may lead to long-term financial starvation."[18] If no money is provided, the librarian must decide whether and how much the library can afford to invest in the new program. If money is provided, some estimate will be required of the effects of the program in future years. Maintaining rationality and objectivity in the fact of faculty pressure is frequently difficult, but a stand must be made if other goals are not to be undermined.

Investment in improvement or in depth is more easily defensible, though frequently much misunderstood as resistance to increasing the breadth of the library's plan. Long-term development of this kind is, however, the surest measurement of the health of a library's programs, since it indicates purposive spending. It may respond to changes in existing academic programs, or result from an overhaul of the collections. Its aim may be to replace old or wornout editions, to complete back sets of serials or to purchase reprints for out-of-print material long-sought but not obtained. It may also result from new talent in either departmental or library staff, which revives a somewhat moribund program and makes new investment profitable. Whatever the reason, these kinds of collection-building allocations are frequently the most profitable both for the library and for the institution. Allocations made for such a purpose should be as generous and as free of restrictions as possible, though all participants will realize that the program may have to extend over more than one year.

The library-related factors begin with the existing situation, which carries with it some overwhelming imperatives. The most significant of these relates to the division of expenditure between subscriptions and other purchases. Coupled with this, the next factor, differential inflation rates among the various areas, may perforce play the single largest role in shaping the library materials budget. The response to this problem may well be the most significant policy decision made in the course of the year. For most of the period 1950–1970, most libraries experienced budget growth sufficient to allow the placing of new subscriptions almost without control. When money became tight, many libraries found that these subscriptions had grown to account for a very high proportion of all expenditures. In some cases the proportion was as high as 90 percent. Despite frequent allegations to the contrary, it is not true that the faculty will gladly forgo other purchases if the subscriptions can be maintained. Nor is it possible, given the average rate of annual cost increase, roughly 15 percent, to increase the library materials budget sufficiently rapidly even to cope with the indefinite maintenance of all subscriptions.

The second group of library factors relates to the program of the library itself. Formulae based solely on academic programs fail to correlate these with such library activities as reserve books or reference, both of which are multidisciplinary. Similarly, the duplication factor necessitated by the existence of multiple service locations cannot be overlooked. In large libraries, moreover, significant expenditures are required to support nonpublic activities such as acquisitions, cataloging or interlibrary loan. Here the question to be considered is whether the library can best afford a second set of Mansell or the time taken by the catalog staff in walking to and from the public area where it is housed, together with the displacement of the public user that is entailed.

Finally, there has to be a kind of "reality" factor. If the academic profile shows an immense investment in education students, which would result in a very large share of the library materials budget, yet at the same time use has been consistently low for years, except for reserves, and the numbers of books published each year that are likely to be requested could not begin to expend the theoretical proportion of the budget available, then "reality" must say the allocation is absurd and should be reduced. This decision may be regarded as subjective (but it must be remembered it is not a judgement about the quality of the program), yet it represents precisely the necessary managerial interpretation of the statistics. Other kinds of factors may indicate the need for such reality judgements. A rare books program, for example, while an extremely desirable quality program is, of its nature, a luxury, by reason both of cost and of low usage. It would be misuse of money if, in a tight budget, a high allocation were made to such a program. The more correct course would be to plan for the use of savings or other special monies, or to recognize some priority in its right to call upon reserved funds in the case of especially important requests. There may, however, be situations in which higher expenditure is easily justifiable, as perhaps during the period when a new art history graduate program is being implemented. A further situation that must be taken into account arises from the fact that delivery of purchases is normally considerably later than the time of ordering. Orders are usually encumbered at the time the order is placed, putting a kind of lien upon the funds so as to ensure that money will be available to pay for the order when it arrives. Because ordering is a continuous process, some orders placed in one fiscal year will not arrive until the next. Some institutions allow the money represented by such encumbrances to be carried forward when it is placed in escrow, and gradually reduced to zero as the material is received. Most do not. In those cases either the encumbrances are transferred to the new fiscal year or the library must cancel and reorder all materials still desired. Whatever the procedure, the purchases represented by these encumbrances are distortions in the planned expenditures for one or more years, and some modification may have to be made to accommodate them. In the case where encumbrances are carried forward, but not the money, care must be taken to see that the allocation takes account of this situation and does not, for instance, allocate less money than is already encumbered. This process may, then, be characterized as one of relating the artifical results of any statistical analysis to the current situation, with all its political and economic implications.

The result of the foregoing considerations should be a library materials budget allocation which reflects both practical and philosophical concerns, but above all it should be one which responds to the needs of the institution. A likely distribution of expenditures is posited in Table 10.

In more down-to-earth language, however, it is essential that the budget allocation cope adequately with commitments and inflation. Table 8 in Chapter 5 indicated the effects of inflation in gross terms, pointing out that simple maintenance of subscriptions within a fixed budget would increase their share of expenditure from 50 percent to 87.5 percent in a period of four years. The more complex issue to be considered here is what would happen to the internal distribution of this money. The effects of differences in rates of inflation are startling. Without pretence at absolute accuracy, the following rates of price increase may be used to investigate such effects. Areas of science have shown increases ranging between 15 and 26 percent per year in the indexes. An average of 20 percent would be realistic. On the other hand, periodicals in the humanities have ranged between 5 and 15 percent, suggesting an average of 10 percent. Life sciences, which includes health and biology, has averaged about 18 percent. Most others areas have averaged 10 to 15 percent.

Table 10. The State University Libraries.

Distribution by Area of the Budget for Library Materials.

Area	Books	Periodicals	Binding	Total
Arts & Performing Arts[1]	25,000	25,000	3,000	53,000
Humanities	50,000	60,000	6,000	116,000
Social Sciences[2]	50,000	65,000	6,000	121,000
Languages	40,000	45,000	5,000	90,000
Education	10,000	10,000	1,000	21,000
Sciences	25,000	90,000	9,000	124,000
Engineering	20,000	55,000	5,000	80,000
Life Sciences	20,000	70,000	6,500	96,500
Reference	15,000	35,000	5,000	55,000
General[3]	100,000	40,500	3,000	143,000
Reserves	20,000	500	—	20,500
Special Collns.	25,000	4,000	500	29,500
	$400,000	$500,000	$50,000	$950,000

Notes: [1] Includes small Art History Program
[2] Includes Psychology, Documents, Law
[3] Includes Browsing Collection, small blanket order, microforms, both sets and subscriptions, newspapers and areas of general interest to all.

Actual figures for each library can be derived from its own records, but these represent increases roughly in line with those indicated by national indexes. If no change is made in the number of subscriptions, these rates may be applied to arrive at a straight-line projection over a five-year period as shown in Table 11. From this table three lessons may be learned. The first is that where there are several variables, the average of those variables cannot be used as a unique predictor. The difference between $889,727 and

Table 11. Straight-line Projection of Periodical Costs.

Area	Initial Allocation		Annual Price Increase Percent	Allocations Required in Fourth Year	
	Amount	Percent		Amount	Percent
Arts & Performing Arts	25,000	5.0	12	39,337	4.42
Humanities	60,000	12.0	10	89,846	9.87
Social Sciences	65,000	13.0	16	117,691	13.23
Languages	45,000	9.0	12	70,808	7.96
Education	10,000	2.0	12	15,735	1.77
Sciences	90,000	18.0	20	186,624	20.98
Engineering	55,000	11.0	15	96,195	10.81
Life Sciences	70,000	14.0	18	135,714	15.25
Reference	35,000	7.0	15	61,215	6.88
General	40,500	8.0	15	70,834	7.96
Reserves	500	0.1	10	732	0.08
Special Collections	4,000	0.8	15	6,996	0.79
TOTAL	$500,000	100.0		$889,727	100.00

$874,503 is not great absolutely, yet it illustrates the variation possible between generalized and detailed predictions. If science and life sciences had had a greater initial budget the final difference between the two projections would have been even larger. The second is that the distribution of money has now changed considerably, even though the same subscriptions are being maintained. The cost of subscriptions for sciences has risen from $90,000 to $186,624 and the proportion of money spent from 18 to 20.98 percent. The third point is that this change in distribution must affect what other allocations can be made if some formula or its approximation is being used as the basis for distribution. Finally, the figures reveal the cost of keeping a library where it is without any expansion.[19] This kind of deviation from a standard figure must be kept in mind when planning a budget distribution.

At the same time as consideration is given to present commitments for subscriptions, a decision has to be reached on the extent, if any, to which new subscriptions can be placed. The unthinkable has become real, as witness this reference to the plight of the library at the University of British Columbia:

Book buying will be curtailed and the moratorium on new periodical subscriptions will be continued (new subscriptions cannot be placed unless a periodical of equal monetary value is canceled).[20]

The formulation and examination of projected costs, which can then be compared against projected income, is the only way in which to arrive at a realistic future distribution. In its absence, only *ad hoc* decisions can be made. On the basis of the projections some general guidelines can be developed. There has been much discussion of the serial/monograph ratio and, although no consensus has emerged, there appears to be general agreement that the proportion of the total library materials budget spent on serials should not be greater than 60 to 70 percent. Any higher proportion reduces the flexibility of any allocation almost to zero and impairs the capacity of the acquisitions program to respond to genuine needs. Naturally the proportion will differ in specific disciplines. The sciences, for example, are generally much more dependent on serials than are the humanities.

It is essential to remember that the development of the annual allocation of funds for library materials concerns the distribution of actual funds, not of an ideal amount. It is therefore requisite that funds be set aside to meet commitments, but that these commitments always be examined in the light of their long-term budgetary effects. Where funds are insufficient to meet all desires, choices must be made between programs and between kinds of expenditure. If, for example, the total funds available were reduced from $950,000 to $900,000, the impact of serial costs totalling $95,000 would be a great deal more severe. In such a situation it would be almost mandatory to cancel some subscriptions in order to preserve buying capacity for other library materials, while at the same time decisions would have to be made about the intensity of expenditure in individual disciplines.

Because most institutions now must use some kind of contingency budget-planning, libraries frequently receive "one-shot" supplements for the library materials budget, rather than permanent budget adjustments. Incorporating such expectations into the planning and allocation process is extremely difficult because there is usually no way of knowing sufficiently far in advance what amount of additional money is likely to be available and when it will be transferred to the library budget. If, in addition, the institution permits the transfer of savings between categories, money can be made available from salary savings for the library materials budget. Again, it is difficult to predict exactly what sum is likely to be involved, though a conservative estimate is usually possible. The net result, however, of all planning is a substantial increase in estimated or contingent income. If the estimates are incorrect or are vitiated by changes in administrative thinking, the plans fall apart. Nevertheless such planning is now a part of academic life and those responsible for setting up the budget must endeavor to allocate these funds in a way that will minimize the effects of their partial or total loss. As far as possible, guaranteed funds must be used to support essential programs. Among these the acquisitions program must take a high place, since the purchasing of books is a continuous operation and must be planned on a flow basis. Other purchases, such as equipment or renovations can be made from contingent funds, since the number of purchases is likely to be few and is in any case discontinuous. When funds in general are tight, such trade-offs are possible; and allocations for equipment, etc., from regular funds can be reduced. There are merits in such a procedure, but it is dangerous as a permanent practice and must, in any case, be carried on only with the support and agreement of the institution.

When encumbrances, including subscriptions, have been allowed for, the next category of basic support relates to current acquisitions. Arguments concerning blanket orders and approval plans are only tangential to this purpose, since the arguments concern mode rather than result. Whatever the mode employed, the aim is to purchase from current output that which is relevant to the mission of the institution. To date, intensive study has been given only to U.S. publishing, probably because it is the most accessible to statistical treatment and because most U.S. libraries buy local publications more systematically. Studies such as those by Massman and Patterson[21] are very useful in examining the entire range of an institution's purchases, while Brazell[22] provides a useful examination of one field, music, and similar studies will prove helpful both in evaluating a current acquisition program and in examining programs for the improvement of an individual collection. The object of a current acquisitions program should be to provide support for each academic area at the level appropriate to the institution's investment in that area. The establishment of appropriate levels may be burdensome. Those commonly accepted range from comprehensive or exhaustive, to research, to teaching, to basic, the latter when there is no organized program of instruction but representation of the subject matter in the collections is desirable.[23] The amount of money required to support such a program will, of course, vary with the needs and goals of the institution. A frequent objection from faculty, and some librarians, is that their interest is really in older material. Just as frequently it will be discovered that if a regular current acquisitions program had been in action in earlier years, these objections would not be made. Not everything that is published should be bought. Even if it were possible, it would be undesirable, since so much is redundant; but it must be stressed that current publications are most easily acquired within a short while of publication and, so far as can be determined at this time, have their greatest use in the first one or two years after publication.

The next consideration in establishing the library materials budget is that of augmentation. Augmentation of resources is a response to demonstrated need, but it carries qualitative rather than quantitative overtones. Work with standard bibliographies may reveal gaps in existing collections. An academic program in a field new to the library will require substantial investment in older resources, and occasionally the institution from its own funds or from a special grant may provide or earmark funds for establishment purposes. In such instances it is important to remember that this is additional money and should not be seen as substituting for regular support. Other special programs which would qualify could be a plan to overhaul and update the library's reference and bibliography collections or to embark on a plan for microform enrichment by the purchase over a period of major collections.

Certain other kinds of expenditure are essential, such as the replacement of lost, stolen or mutilated resources or the setting aside of money for an exchange program that provides materials unobtainable in any other way.

The object of this process is to produce a budget distribution which provides for each area of expenditure and for each kind, but which is not so rigid that fortuitous circumstances or internal change cannot be accommodated. In particular it must be possible to take care of unplanned increases such as postal charges without having to recast the whole. No initial budget should ever distribute the whole sum available. Whether the reserve is set aside at the beginning of the year or regarded as a first charge on savings, is immaterial so long as it is planned for. The actual distribution will, of course, reflect the organization of the library and may also reflect external constraints such as an institutional requirement that it be possible in year-end reporting to relate library expenditures to academic areas. The individual accounts should be no more in number than is required to meet this goal and should not be so small that the labor of maintaining the records exceeds the value of the fund. It is possible to subdivide accounts by the type of purchase—*e.g.*, microforms, monographs, sets; but such an arrangement is so cumbersome as to be counterproductive. In keeping with the general goal of program budgets, which is to reduce control to the necessary minimum, accounts should be set up to support the exercise of professional judgement in purchasing one kind of material as against another. The only caution that must be observed is in the field of periodical subscriptions, where each purchase is not an isolated transaction but a permanent and increasing commitment of future funds. Each account or fund should be assignable to one person, even if that person in turn works with several others. Such a course makes easier the maintenance of authority, responsibility and accountability.

In all libraries there are funds, large or small, which are predicated. That is, by wish of the donor, or an instruction from the funding source, they are to be spent in a particular manner or within a specified subject field. It is impossible here to cover the whole area of gifts and endowments. Suffice it to say that libraries should discourage gifts which are so specific that it may be impossible to meet the conditions over a period of years,[24] or which would contribute to an undesirable imbalance. The onerous conditions might be that certain persons should approve all purchases or that the purchases must be placed in a certain library, regardless of whether that library's mission is appropriate or not. A one-time gift on such a basis may be no more than a nuisance, but an endowment that produces annual income may more nearly resemble a deadweight than an encouragement to the library. It is surprising how long it can take to spend $1000 (with interest) on books on the American free enterprise system written from an evangelical viewpoint! All gifts and endowments should be represented by allocations which enable expenditures to be made in accordance with the wishes of the original donor. Institutional accounting practice varies, but it is customary to establish either separate funds or a consolidated gift fund. Sometimes there will be a separate fund relating to each office which handles gifts, as for example the alumni office of an individual college within a university. In most cases the library will have to establish a sort of double entry in order both to report back to the donor and to enable purchases to be made by the appropriate library selector or department.

The final result should be a kind of matrix which assigns funds (and the responsibility for them) to selectors and which summarizes them by category and by financial source. An example is cited in Table 12. It is recognized that this or any other method may not be available to or suitable for an individual library, but it illustrates how both divisions can be shown in the presentation of the budget. No distribution will ever satisfy all requirements, whether budgetary or political. On the other hand decisions will always have to be made with reflect the politics of the institution or the imperatives of the budget.

As with all budget plans, the shape of the distribution should not be set so firmly that change is impossible. Whether by the use of general or reserve funds, or by the diversion of savings, it should be possible to allow for unexpected needs or underestimated inflation.

Table 12. Allocation for Life Sciences

AGRIC 101	General Funds (1001)	Resource Funds (3850)	Special Funds	Total
Subscriptions: Perio.	73,995	4,000	—	77,995
Series	1,700	—	—	1,700
Other	10	—	—	10
Subtotal	75,705	4,000	—	79,705
"Books"	11,800	5,000	2,144	18,944
TOTAL	87,505	9,000	2,144	98,649
HELTH 107				
Subscriptions: Perio	32,764	—	—	32,764
Series	2,700	—	—	2,700
Subtotal	35,464	—	—	35,464
"Books"	5,500	2,000	—	7,500
TOTAL	40,964	2,000	—	42,964
UNIT TOTAL	128,469	11,000	2,144	141,613

Source: Taken from the Library Materials Budget, The Pennsylvania State University Libraries, 1975/76.

GOODS AND SERVICES

Although this category is the smallest library outlay, it may be considered the most critical, since from it are purchased the daily operational needs of the library. It is interesting that despite the necessity of supplies, equipment, rental, postage and the like, no direct or indirect mention of this kind of expenditure is made in *Standards for College Libraries,* which may be partial evidence of the apparent fact that such costs are very frequently overlooked in academic planning. Since these costs are among those that have been most affected by inflation and changing technology, such an appearance of disregard is strange. Lack of regard for this budgetary need has serious implications for the library.

In this area, historical information is of critical importance. The majority of expenditure items follow a fairly consistent pattern from year to year. Changes are dependent on changes in the library program or in technology. The number of catalog cards purchased, for example, reflect the number of books cataloged.

The latter number tends to be fairly constant and, if not, can readily be deduced from the amount of money available for purchases. In other words, it is not a factor subject to violent fluctuations, unless the whole budget is so affected and the appropriate amount must therefore be allowed. Occasionally, however, a quite new factor, such as the use of terminals for data-base searching, may be added to the library program. If no allowance has been made for the total recovery or amortization of costs, then provision for this expenditure must come either at the expense of other items or from additional money. Knowing how much paper, how many Princeton files, were purchased and how much was spent on postage or telephones, etc., makes the consideration of such questions much simpler.

In the same way, by the examination of the record it is possible to determine the fixed and the variable portions of each subcategory and to calculate what expansion is necessary or what reduction could be made without disruptive side effects. Depending on the amount of money available, all, or only some, of the necessities may be supportable. In the latter case the decision has to be made whether to call on funds from elsewhere in the budget or to reduce all or some of the items. It is at this stage that the degree of flexibility in the use, for example, of savings becomes very important. The decision may have to be made that all equipment purchases have to be made from savings.

Although Dougherty and Heinritz, in their book *Scientific Management of Library Operations,* are basically concerned with the analysis of expenditure rather than the setting up of budgets, the chapter on costs contains some very pertinent observations. Depreciation is not normally included directly in the budgetary planning of institutions, yet it is a factor that cannot be ignored.

> The cost of equipment has been increasing for many years. The cost of replacing an item when it is worn out or obsolete will probably be higher than the original cost.[25]

For the most part, educational institutions, including libraries, simply absorb such costs into current operating expenses. Where the increase is substantial and the purchase necessary, this may place the library in a very awkward situation. Consideration of standard tables of depreciation will enable the librarian to estimate when replacements are likely to be necessary. For instance, this year a half-dozen microform readers may have to be replaced; while next year there may be a need for fifty or more replacement chairs. Naturally the replacement should be made only if it is necessary, but it cannot be postponed indefinitely. If the need coincides with a bad budget year, lack of forward planning may render replacement impossible.

They also recommend caution in the stockpiling of supplies, both because there are storage costs and because of possible obsolescence. Storage costs are not generally direct and visible, but the space used might well have been used to better purpose and is in that sense an indirect cost. In this age, when automation is changing many library activities and when standardization is reducing individuality, all supply items should be examined for current usefulness. Not only is it undesirable to hoard forms which may shortly not be needed, it is highly desirable to take the occasion of renewal to examine forms or cards or letterheads for redesign. It is frequently possible to amalgamate two existing forms into one, and it should be possible to eliminate personal names from letterheads rather than junk the stationery when the person named leaves the library. Such possibilities should be taken into account when allocating funds.

Mention was made in Chapter 4 of the alternatives presented by renting or purchasing equipment and of the associated maintenance costs. The costs of these transactions for the budget year must be calculated carefully and the effects of any planned changes taken into account. If, during the course of the year, it will be necessary to renegotiate a long-term rental, to add, change or take out certain machines, the results of these activities must be provided for. New equipment carries with it the need for further maintenance contracts. Sometimes there is a period of warranty, during which no maintenance is charged. In the case of a computer system or other equally sophisticated equipment, the determination of the date a warranty begins or expires may become the subject of considerable debate. In other instances, maintenance is not charged until the equipment is unpacked and put to use. Here again the actual date for the commencement of the service may be disputed and require negotiation. The amounts of money involved are frequently trifling, but in the case of a computer where the costs may be calculated in hundreds of dollars a day, the outcome of the negotiation is of critical importance. Exactness in the identification of all costs is required of any responsible administrator and should be standard practice within a library.

For many machines such as photocopiers there are alternative rental plans, usually based on volume of use. Past history will determine when they are to come up for renewal, but the budget should be set up with likely changes in mind. Underutilized machines should be scheduled for replacement with cheaper ones, and added capacity sought where necessary. In the same way there are alternative plans for smaller items such as typewriters and a decision must be made on the one most suitable for the library. This does not mean a uniform plan unless the institution requires it. The frequency of maintenance should be suited to the amount of use. A typewriter that is seldom used may not need even a quarterly inspection, but those in a typing pool may need one monthly. Provision for irregular or nonessential expenditures should be based on policy decisions. Except in bad years, they will tend to remain constant or to reflect some allowance for inflation. Care must be taken, however, to allow for decisions made by the institution. For example, the mileage allowance for car travel is frequently adjusted every year or two, in line with federal decisions. This allowance applies whether the car used is private or belongs to the institution. In the former case, it is possible to decide to provide a lower rate of reimbursement. In the latter case, a charge to the library budget at the standard rate will be automatic. Such arrangements, which usually do not require the presentation of expense accounts, lead to the feeling that there is no cost, although the automatic debits add up remarkably quickly. This is so for any transaction that requires merely the entry of debits and credits in the university's books of account, and care must be taken to provide sufficient funds for expected expenditures, or to provide the necessary controls to regulate expenditure.

Expenditures for travel, staff-development, research of publications are handled differently by different institutions. Knowledge of what is available and how the institution accounts for such expenditures is necessary to set up the appropriate divisions in the budget. The control of these expenditures will differ, but it must be possible to identify them correctly. Forward estimate of likely costs is quite difficult since the impact will be variable. A further source of difficulty can be the requirement, on occasion, for matching funds from the library budget to support funds from other sources, whether internal or external to the institution. In such a situation it may be necessary to extract expenditures from several subcategories and place them in a separate account. For instance, a grant received in support of a publication may include money for travel, for typing, for the cost of printing and for reimbursement of overhead costs. Each of these may in turn be differentially distributed between sources of funds.

Certain kinds of expenditures, which are not strictly for goods and services, may be charged to this category. One of these is the payment of unemployment compensation. Here the chief requirement is to be aware of changes in federal regulations regarding the length of time during which compensation is payable. It is almost impossible, because of the complexity of the law and the fact that each case is different, to be able to predict exactly what amount the library may have to pay; but since it is mandated by law, the necessary payments will have to be made and any extra money needed will be a first charge on reserves or savings. It is prudent, therefore, to establish a separate account.

Many institutions have established a separate category of expenditure to cover hiring expenses—usually for faculty positions only, but others may be included as well. In part this action has been in response to the greater need for accountability to external agencies in pursuit of affirmative action goals, but it is important to realize how much it costs to recruit new faculty and staff members. The establishment of a separate account covering travel expenses, advertisements and the like makes it easier to monitor the program. The total cost will, of course, reflect the needs of the year in question. For that reason the initial estimate will seldom relate very closely to the year-end total. Because these costs relate to vacant positions for which no salary is being paid, it is logical to support them from those savings. Even so, some expenses are incurred in most cases before the vacancy begins, and an initial provision should be made from regular funds to tide the library over the first few months of the year. As with many other similar expenses, it is highly desirable to centralize their accounting, rather than to distribute them among departments or other budgetary subdivisions. Individual costs can be charged back, if necessary, at the end of the year, but it is essential to know, during the year, the total cost, particularly in order to simplify transfers if these are needed.

DISCRETIONARY OR RESERVE FUNDS

If this kind of fund is provided, it is necessary to have in it at the beginning of the year sufficient to cover likely expenditures during the year. Likely payments will be differences in salaries for new appointees, permanent or temporary transfers to funds that are exhausted before the end of the year, and special allocations for the purchase of collections, major equipment or perhaps for a temporary appointment. In some cases this will be the fund from which anniversary increments for clerical positions are paid. It is important in all cases to distinguish between temporary and permanent budget adjustments since these will affect the year-end balance. In order to give this a more concrete meaning, the imaginary series of transactions in Table 13 illustrates the effects of such transfers. From this table it is clear that without a further infusion of funds, there would not be enough to cover the regular anniversary increases for clerical staff in the next year. If no extra funds were available to the library it would be necessary when setting up the budget to transfer from other permanent funds sufficient money to cover such expenses. In actual fact, temporary money would flow in and out of this account, making it even more difficult to assess the effect on the permanent portion. It is clear, however, that substantial use of such contingency funds for permanent purposes deprives the fund of its ability to provide for emergencies or other

Table 13. Contingency Fund Record.

Balance at beginning of year	$60,000
Temporary transfers to library materials	−10,000
	50,000
Permanent transfers to salaries (increase for two positions)	−3,000
	47,000
Transfers of savings from vacant positions filled at lower rates (permanent)	+6,000
	53,000
Permanent transfers to clerical positions (anniversary increases)	−25,000
	28,000
Permanent transfer to goods and services (increased maintenance)	−5,000
	23,000
Temporary transfer to hiring expenses	−2,000
	21,000
Permanent transfer to newly created position	−15,000
Balance at end of year	$ 6,000

Note: Since a total of $48,000 has been transferred out as against only $6,000 transferred in, the permanent fund has been depleted by $42,000. Therefore the initial balance in the next year will be only $18,000.

special situations where sums of money are required. It may then be necessary to adjust this budgetary item at the expense of goods and services or library materials.

THE ACCOUNTING STRUCTURE

The preceding discussion has suggested general lines upon which funds should be allocated rather than a specific set of accounts. The accounts which result from these considerations should be as simple as is consonant with the achievement of the goals of the library, yet detailed enough to respond to planning and management information needs. They must, of course, also be in accord with the general policies of the institution, which usually assigns both nomenclature and coding to all financial activities. A sample of such accounts appears in Rogers and Weber.[26] Of course, whether or not such a detailed allocation is made formally, it will be done informally or by internal suballocation.

Where it is necessary, the library must modify or go beyond the institutional structure. It is, in fact, usual to do so in the case of library materials, where it is usually of no consequence to the central accounting office whether a book is bought for sociology or economics. Because it is, however, important to the library, the necessary accounting structure must be created. It is possible, though, that these accounts would have to be so arranged as to enable reports to be made that relate expenditure to the organization of the institution. In some cases, too, the funding authority requires a specific structure. Sometimes such a requirement can be met by reformatting the year-end reports, which, of course, implies the ability to extract the appropriate information from a differently structured set of accounts. Finally, reports for federal and other authorities frequently require a different division of expenditure, the details of which may change each year. Not all such requirements can be met without inordinate expense, but the implication is clear that the accounts must be set up in accordance with the need for planning, control and reporting.

NOTES
1. Summers, p. 1175.
2. Rogers and Weber (1971), p. 165.
3. Allen (1972), Appendix A, p. 29.

4. *Ibid.*, pp. 19–27.
5. Fairholm, pp. 335–338.
6. Drake, pp. 53–59.
7. Marchant, pp. 449–457.
8. Schad, p. 155.
9. *Ibid.*, pp. 158–159.
10. McGrath, pp. 356–369.
11. Massman and Patterson, p. 84.
12. "Standards for College Libraries" (October, 1975), p. 290. Emphasis added.
13. Dix, p. 257.
14. McGrath, Huntsinger and Barker, p. 62.
15. Schad, p. 159.
16. Axford, "An Approach to Performance Budgeting at the Florida Atlantic University Library," pp. 99 and 103. This reference illustrates the use of existing ratios or weighting to modify a formula.
17. "Standards for College Libraries" (October, 1975), pp. 299–301.
18. Barnes (1971), p. 106.
19. Baumol and Marcus (1973, pp. 56–57) discuss the problem of rising costs and conclude "that society can, if it chooses, meet these rising costs." The problem faced by most libraries in the seventies arises from that conditional clause, a further reminder that political motives as much as or even more than economic ones control the setting of budgets.
20. "Student Wage Hike Forces Cuts at B.C. Library" (March 15, 1976), *Library Journal*, 101: 773.
21. Massman and Patterson, pp. 83–88.
22. Brazell, Jr., pp. 110–120.
23. The activities of the Collection Development Committee of the Resources Section, Resources and Technical Services Division, American Library Association, in producing guidelines and providing a forum for the discussion of collection development are of great importance. All interested librarians should keep in close touch with the Committee's reports and guidelines.
24. Rogers and Weber (1971), p. 117.
25. Dougherty and Heinritz (1966), p. 158.
26. Rogers and Weber (1971), pp. 100–102.

Chapter 10

Coping with Change

Revision of a plan involves considerable reworking of the unit's labors of love.
(Robins, 1973)

With the end of the affluent sixties, the situation has become increasingly common in which expected revenues cannot meet all the costs of proposed or even existing programs. The reasons for this are many and have been examined in depth by the Carnegie Commission and others. Whatever they are, administrators are now faced with a quite new problem, the setting of priorities among programs which in earlier years would have been funded without question as equally worthy of support. In the beginning, this cost squeeze called forth a variety of responses including emergency measures such as hiring freezes or substantial cuts across the board. But, as administrators have had time to gain perspective, there has been a shift to less draconian ways of controlling the budget. These have usually extended the process to a wider range of program or unit heads, placing the emphasis on "the need for accountability of programs, and for more effective, efficient use of funds."[1]

Institutions of higher learning, whether private or public, differ in many ways from corporate enterprises. The most significant of these for the purposes of this book is that they do not generate income, or at least not in the same way as business or industry do. The fees charged to students are undoubtedly significant as income, but in most institutions they are insufficient to support even the teaching program. Further sources of income such as gifts or endowment income, grants in support of research or legislated income are necessary to maintain the enterprise. Those who must deal with the disbursement of funds are usually not involved in fund-raising and consequently are not as aware as the average entrepreneur of the vital link between income and expenditure.

This separation has further important implications for budget-makers, because it is almost or nearly impossible to establish clear links between input and output. The measurement of educational output is so complex that the assignment of production costs almost defies analysis. In the halcyon days, this was of no great consequence. As income shrinks, however, it becomes more and more necessary to measure and to quantify in order to allocate expenditures. Pressure is exerted to "increase productivity," which usually translates as higher numbers of students in a class per teacher. Secondarily, efforts may be made to weed out weak or "unproductive" programs. Unpleasant as these activities may be for those affected, they are usually able to have some say about academic changes; and whatever the appearance, everyone recognizes that the college will continue its teaching program.

As has frequently been mentioned earlier in this book, libraries are in a unique position among academic units in that, for the most part, they do not define the limits of their program. Collection building, reference services or circulation services are generated in response to institutional need. Moreover, all these aspects of library service link together into a program. Whereas a college can, and sometimes does, decide to discontinue teaching in a given field, libraries can at best discontinue marginal services whose budget impact is small. In consequence, the likely result of shrinking funds is more likely to be a tightening up, than a lopping off, of services. As a general principle tautness is necessary to ensure the wise expenditure of money.[2] It should not, of course, mean such tightness that the individual units are unable to function at all. If the level of budgetary support has indeed sunk that low, then there must be reductions in services offered. The attitude engendered by the sixties was that good service was dependent upon a bountiful supply of money—in short, that money could solve all problems. As a carry-over, the attitude is still found that a unit cannot do its task because it is inadequately funded. The pressure now is to seek alternatives by changing the methods of working or by substituting one task or service for another. Although the agonizing decisions that must be made in setting up a budget reflecting reduced funds appear to be a crisis of great magnitude, they are also evidence of a longer and much more important process of readjustment. Libraries have, as Galvin puts it, "not been, and generally are not now, in a particularly strong position to respond effectively to the new requirements of fiscal accountability."[3] In particular the development of efficient measures of activity has lagged behind need, the library having traditionally been perceived as self-justifying.

Such a background does little to prepare librarians for handling budget reductions, and any budget that does not cover the full effects of inflation requires some corresponding program reduction. If measures of activity, such as have been discussed earlier, are available the librarian at least has some place to start. Trends and areas of particular pressure can be established and some idea gained of the likely future shape of the library in different sets of circumstances. Although this kind of prognostication may be regarded as a "what if" process, it is necessary at least to guess at the future effects of different combinations of decisions. Those that are totally unacceptable can then be discarded; and the others given more careful consideration, in the search for a future plan realistic both in terms of budget and of programs.

The temptation is always present to respond in simplistic terms. If the budget is cut 5 percent, then all programs must take a 5 percent cut. Such a response is an abdication of administrative responsiblity. The process of deciding on reduced allocations is as important as any other part of the budget process and must be equally program related. The actual formal division of the money available into specific accounts is less important than it is to ensure that the process of doing so takes into account the needs and priorities of the library. It is this process which relies most heavily on good statistical and financial reporting, where different needs and different levels of need can be identified.

The first consideration must be to provide for activities that must be continued, the next to withdraw funds from activities that are to be reduced or discontinued. What is left must be apportioned as nearly as possible in accordance with the priorities of the library. This sounds relatively simple, but in fact consists of a great number of interdependent decisions, some of which are immediate, some delayed and some contingent. The simple solution, a library-wide cut of a certain magnitude, overlooks the different levels of intensities of activities and minimizes the very real differences in size between different units. It is impossible, for example, to save 5 percent of the costs of a program that consists of one staff member, a small amount of supplies and an allocation for library materials without improperly penalizing that program because all the savings would have to be effected in library materials and supplies, thus effectively rendering the program unable to operate. Reductions must therefore be practical in their application. It is also possible that even in a time when the total amount of funds is reduced that some library activities are increasing or that certain inescapable costs will increase. The example was cited earlier of the effects of retaining serial subscriptions intact on the distribution and total of other kinds of library materials purchases. The same applies to any area where standing still implies greater expenditure because of inflation.

The actions undertaken by the Pennsylvania State University to meet inflationary pressures following a general budget cut may be examined by way of illustration. Table 14 summarizes the zero-budget changes made in the middle of 1974. It is to be realized that before this activity a percentage of the budget had been returned to the central administration. Most of that was represented by vacant positions, in accordance with the university's instructions. It was found necessary to reestablish two positions to deal with work-load increases, and other changes were necessary to meet inflation, in the case of maintenance and rental costs or mandated wage-rate increases in the case of wages. The only area in which there was spare money was "books and binding," which had consequently to

Table 14. Adjustments made to Zero Budget, 1974/75.
The Pennsylvania State University Libraries.

	Increase	Decrease
670–94 Allocation fund Increase from $11,918 to $31,918	$20,000	
670–70 Salaries		
Establish academic position: Rank—Senior Asst., Plan A	16,056	
Clerk, Grade 5 (5C)	6,528	
Grad. Assts. (To allow for Gr. 6 appointments)	818	
Wages—(Increase from $231,000 to $281,000)	50,000	
Allotment—NonBook (Increase from $205,573 to $265,573)	60,000	
Allotment—Books & Binding		$143,402
TOTAL	$153,402	$143,402
Sales Income (Increase from $38,908 to $48,908)	10,000	
NET	$143,402	$143,402

be "robbed" with the clear understanding that library materials should have first call on temporary funds such as salary savings. The transfer of funds into the allocation fund was required by circumstances such as these noted in the consideration of contingency funds in Chapter 9, notably provision for payment of anniversary increases to clerks. These actions implied a decision to hold steady in all areas except the one critical area in which extra staff were needed (a branch library) and to reduce significantly the acquisitions program. In addition, though maintenance and rental cost increases had been provided for, purchases in all other areas of goods and services would be reduced by the effects of inflation. The changes, taken as a whole, represent a decision in favor of services and against collections. This decision appeared to be in accordance with the general priorities, at that time, of both the library and the institution. The figures in Table 14 also represent gross amounts only. The internal distribution of remaining funds was still made in accordance with the needs of the library's programs, and adjustments continued to be made internally in the course of the year to reflect the goals and aspirations of the various library units.

The degree of fund-shifting shown in the cited example is only possible within the zero-based budget concept, and even then it is frequently subject to a variety of limitations. This kind of adjustment differs from the changes caused by a sudden increase or decrease of funds during the year because it is permanent, not temporary. Also it is not the kind of adjustment that can be repeated frequently, since it tends to reduce flexibility to nothing.

Nevertheless, the aim of any major budget adjustment should be to realign funds in accordance with the new necessities of policy. If realignment can be carried out by the library, it is much more likely to remain supportive of the services offered. Consultation and cooperation in arriving at the new budget will strengthen its acceptance. Change in and of itself is not a bad thing. It forces the reconsideration of basic principles as well as of frills, and presents libraries with a challenge. People frequently say "the budget won't let me do this or that." What they usually mean is "I want more money and can't get it." Both these statements indicate that the speaker has given up and is using the nonexistence of budgetary support as an excuse for not making decisions. After all the budget "does not restrict or allow—people do these."[4]

The budget is only the summary on paper of many decisions, some of which are temporary and some of which may likely prove mistaken. It is subject to amendment and its various parts correspond to the multitude of activities that will occur during the year. Those activities result from the managerial and professional decisions of the library staff. The ledgers simply record the fiscal results of those activities. The record must be consulted to see where the money is and where it might go, but if policies are changed and new priorities decided on, the record will then reflect those changes.

Because library budgets are generally unitary, it is not always realized that the transfer of a position from one unit to another, even though it does not result in any monetary change, is a budget change. This is so because more of the commodity time has been added to one operation, thereby changing its price, and, it is hoped, improving its product or its productivity. With static or declining budgets, such actions become more common. Such changes may be termed voluntary—*i.e.*, there was the option not to make the transfer.

Involuntary changes are those that must be made in response to external forces. There is still some choice in the manner of response, but change of some kind is inevitable. This is particularly true in such matters as basic wage rates, or union wage negotiations, where the decision is outside the control of the unit administrator. If the basic wage rate is increased, there are only three possible responses. The administrator can find the necessary extra money to maintain employment, or reduce the number of hours of employment, or find a combination of both. The likeliest result is the third alternative, but in the case of union negotiations the only option may be the first. Whatever the result, these involuntary changes require voluntary changes to maintain a balanced budget.

In the process of adjustment, many things once considered impossible come to pass. One dramatic change has been the realization that some services must be charged for. While the discussion, in fact, concerns data bases, Gardner and Wax[5] offer some comments that should be more widely pondered by library administrators. As they suggest, the advent of a new and expensive service, at a time when there was no money to support the principle of free access, forced libraries to consider the question of user fees. When to this is added the increasingly common charge for interlibrary loans and the addition of service charges for photocopying, it is clear that libraries have begun anew to examine the hitherto sacred relationship of borrower and library. This is a response to change both social and technological we may expect to see extend through the next decade. More than ever then, librarians must use fiscal control as a means of establishing program control in the interests of the priorities they have determined.

NOTES
1. Robins (1973), p. 5.
2. Rogers and Weber (1971), pp. 165, 177, 213. These brief discussions of budgeting for various library divisions stress that a certain amount of pressure is necessary in the interests of efficiency.
3. Galvin (September 15, 1976), p. 1835.
4. Robins (1973), p. 69.
5. Gardner and Wax, pp. 1827–1832.

Chapter 11

Monitoring the Budget

> *The library shall maintain such internal accounts as are necessary for approving its invoices for payment, monitoring its encumberances* (sic), *and evaluating the flow of its expenditures.*
> ("Standards for College Libraries," 8,3.)

Whether the sets of accounts are simple or complex, a library requires the authority, information and control that is represented by those accounts. Authority to charge expenditures against specific accounts carries with it the responsibility for seeing that those expenditures are properly so charged. There is often a feeling that budgetary control is something carried out by some central office. This is not so: "budget control starts with those responsible for each budgetary unit."[1] This does not necessarily mean only those who are formally responsible for budgets according to the institutions's coded distribution, but anyone who is given the task of supervising expenditure on time and things. With this responsibility goes accountability for the results. Without information as to what has already been spent or encumbered, no one is in a position to decide on further purchases. Without the control that is represented by the allocation of specific sums for specific purposes, there would be no way of ensuring that the library fulfill its goals for the year. The monitoring of its progress toward these ends requires the assistance and cooperation of many people within the library.

Despite the best efforts of administrators, it is not always possible for the budget to be in final form at the beginning of the fiscal year. At one extreme, the legislature may not have passed a budget, thus requiring that agencies act within the constraints imposed by temporary, partial funding. At the other, in an institution where balances represented by encumbrances may not be carried forward, but must either be canceled or taken into account in setting up the book allocations for the next year, it is never possible to prepare a final distribution until the accounts for the preceding year are completed. Even such matters as quarterly crediting of interest on endowment funds may delay the preparation of final figures. In most cases it is desirable to provide temporary figures, both to enable essential expenditures to be made and to allow the accounts themselves to be set up. Clearly such temporary figures must be within the likely final figures for each account, and may be controlled either by the kinds of expenditures allowed, or the portion of the year they represent. Such a procedure is, incidentally, more for the library's own benefit than for the institution, where expenditures are usually controlled only by gross amounts. Of course, in a real financial crisis, special instructions would be issued establishing what kinds of expenditures would be allowed or disallowed and the library, like other units, would have to conform. Even in ordinary circumstances it is undesirable to allow expenditures to accumulate in an account which may not be funded to the amount originally planned. Care must therefore be taken in the initial period of each new fiscal year to provide for essential expenditures while holding back in areas where either funding or plans are uncertain.

The longer the period of uncertainty, however, the more difficult it will become to carry out successfully the plans for the year. This is particularly true in the purchasing of equipment items, where there are usually more complex preorder procedures and also long delivery schedules. It is, however, true as well of books and other materials, where the diversities both of source and method of purchase are great, and where the average unit price is low, thus making it essential to maintain a fairly regular distribution of activity throughout the year. If this cannot be done and money is released late in the year, not only does this cause bunching that will be reflected later in other departments, but it militates against careful choice and encourages wasteful purchasing of available, expensive items.

As soon as either temporary or permanent budget distribution has been determined, its contents must be passed on to those who will be responsible for handling the various funds. Who these will be is determined by the organization of the library. Some libraries are decentralized to the extent that almost all funds are subdivided by department or branch. Some retain control within the central library administration. Two areas, where responsibility for the handling of funds is usually widespread, are wages and libary materials. This is so because in both these areas the funds can be better utilized in furtherance of program goals by decentralization than by close central control. Responsibility for the actual payment of all salaries is usually centralized and decentralized control over budgets for full-time employees would at best be nugatory—a matter of information rather than power. It could, however, become a very live issue, if the library were forced to make staff reductions or to transfer positions between departments. It is, therefore, not recommended that authority over personnel budgets be removed from the central library administration. Since consultation in any change is the accepted form, attention must be paid to individual unit concerns, but it must be possible for the administration to react to change as freely as possible.

At first sight it seems reasonable to disperse accounts for supplies and the like to each area or unit. A moment's consideration will, however, reveal the fallacy. Most supplies are used in common. Is it reasonable to set up twenty accounts for paper? What happens when Department A runs out of envelopes halfway through the year and has no money left in its account, while Department B is hoarding its money to buy a set of special folders not available until later in the year? Even more cogent is the problem of whose responsibility major items should be. Is the Catalog Department owner of and responsible for catalog cabinets for the public catalog? It must also be considered that delivery for such a cabinet may take thirteen months, effectively spans two budget years, and requires very careful advance planning. Similar questions could be raised concerning almost every kind of payment for goods and services. It should be known where the expenses are incurred, but responsibility for their control should remain with the central administration of the library.

Special problems occur where there are several sources of funds. A simple example is the case of a joint appointment, shared by the library and another administrative unit. A more complex one might be a rare-books or special library where some income is from endowments or other special sources, and where plans for expenditure require the concurrence of an advisory board or similar organ. In such cases the control function must allow for the necessary consultation and sharing of information during the year. It is particularly important to be aware of accounts that require the signature of more than one administrative officer and to give them special treatment.

Monitoring is carried out on several levels. At the basic level, it consists of inspecting all orders and invoices to make sure they are prepared according to the appropriate institutional procedure and applied to the correct account. Routine as this instruction may appear to be, it is essential that all personnel in the library who are responsible for the handling of financial accounts and forms be kept up to date regarding procedures. Equally, no greater number of personnel than is absolutely necessary should be involved. For convenience or as a result of a permissive attitude, this number is frequently allowed to grow until it becomes impossible for any one administrator to ensure adherence to policies and procedures. A very common example of such laxity is the existence of numerous change funds, which are in effect petty cash funds without the controls that go with the formal establishment of such a fund. The same rule of parsimony applies to the number of persons allowed to authorize expenditures from book-fund allocations. Where too many people have access to one fund it becomes impossible either to plan or to control expenditure. The fewer exceptions that are made the better will be the control, and the exceptions must be based upon clear need rather than convenience or seniority. As an example, if at all possible, all invoices for book funds should be handled by one person or by the person's delegates. If this rule is applied, then the accounts department can and should refuse any invoice from other sources, thus ensuring that information on purchases and expenditures is channeled only through the proper authority. In effect, at some final point, before leaving the library, all invoices and other financial documents are checked for accuracy. It is better and less costly if they reach this point correct in all respects. The number of monitoring activities that must be carried out at this level is infinite. A system that reduces to the lowest possible number the possibility of differences in interpretation is guaranteed to save both time and money.

Similarly, in most institutions, certain signatures only are recognized as authorizing payment. The decision as to who shall have this authority depends upon internal circumstances. In general, however, the more discretionary the nature of the expenditure the higher will be the level of approval. For example, travel reimbursement is usually subject to complex rules, which require the exercise of judgement; and it is also subject to budgetary constraints, which require that care be taken in achieving some fairness of distribution. In such a case, wide distribution of authority to sign could easily result in unintentional abuse or budgetary overruns; and it is customary to require that authorization for travel reimbursements be restricted to the head librarian. A different kind of restriction may be exercised, either within the library or in the institution as a whole, and relates to the monetary value of a transaction. Any purchase of equipment, for example, for $1,000 in value may require the approval of a vice-president, or may have to be put out on bid. Libraries, in general, are allowed a fair degree of freedom in placing orders for library materials. This freedom is allowed on the basis of the librarian's exercise of professional judgement and therefore requires that the librarian act responsibly. That responsibility includes care in the selection of dealers, in the handling of money and in the choice of objects for expenditure. The library must, therefore, have internal rules that require a certain concentration of responsibility in the authorization of expensive purchases. In these days of constricted budgets and increasing prices, this usually implies restriction; and the approval of some group or committee may be required before expensive individual purchases are made.

The accounts themselves provide essential planning information. The intelligent use of this information will help the library to make the best use of the resources available. The record over the year indicates whether or not plans are being met and suggests when remedial action must be taken. In this context it is true, as noted by Rogers and Weber, "that accurate records are essential for management just as much as for accounting purposes."[2] While this is not meant to suggest that accuracy to the last cent is necessary for management purposes, it is clear that gross errors, slowness in reporting either encumbrances or expenditures and mistakes in fund attribution would render meaningless any planning effort. The whole goal of any set of accounts should be to present in as accurate and up-to-date a form as possible the financial status of the library.

It is convenient for the purposes of examination once again to divide this review into three parts, each of which deals with a major category of library expenditure.

PERSONNEL-RELATED EXPENSES

As distinct from formulae that establish the desired number in the work force, or analysis that examines the distribution of tasks among that work force, this section is concerned with the fiscal records that must form the basis of that analysis. It would be easy to assume that records concerning personnel being centralized in most institutions are therefore correct,[3] but this assumption overlooks the complexity that has gathered around any records having to do with personnel salaries. Moreover, it is becoming more and more common for the responsibility for initiating personnel decisions to be decentralized, which places squarely on the library administration the task of ensuring accuracy.

At the beginning of each fiscal period it is customary to prepare a new budget statement, which usually includes a statement of individual salaries. Because the budget must be prepared at a specific time, any changes since that time will not be shown; and these corrections should be made immediately to the printed budget, working from prior documentation (*e.g.*, payroll change forms, budget amendments or the like). These changes may consist of such relatively simple transactions as the replacement of one typist by another, but may also include new positions added, changes in the grade of positions or changes in salary rates. Inspection may also reveal simple errors, *e.g.*, the wrong classification of a position, or the assignment of an incorrect faculty rank. Despite the best efforts of administrators, such errors may persist for years—even, or perhaps particularly, in a computerized system. They may seem inconsequential, but to the person whose retirement plan or status they threaten, they are clearly of consequence. The importance, too, of being correct when working for affirmative action and other personnel goals cannot be overestimated. A simple error of this nature could result in a substantial claim at law.

Having established the correctness of the initial budget with care, the budget officer must show the same care in maintaining correct records for the year. The decisions will be made by the officer responsible for personnel management, usually in consultation with the budget officer, but in any case the budget officer is responsible for checking the accuracy of the figures and affirming compliance with institutional regulations. The commonest situations affecting personnel records are terminations, new appointments, the creation or cancellation of positions and salary changes. These all have in common the fact that they affect both the total and the distribution of personnel costs. A related topic is the handling of savings that accrue from vacant positions or other changes.

In a large library there is a substantial turnover of staff each year. The greater number is in clerical or similar positions, but the library profession has long been characterized as mobile and a turnover of about 10 percent a year would not be surprising. Each termination (and usually the replacement) requires the establishment of certain facts: (1) the date of termination, which may or may not be the last day of service and which depends on accrued leave, unused sick-leave, etc., and may be complicated by institutional rules on such matters as maternity leave; (2) the exact rate of pay, which may sound strange, since the present salary is already known, but which, because a long period of notice may be required, may extend past a time when an automatic increase is made or a new salary scale comes into effect; and (3) any other information pertinent to future expenses, such as a possible unemployment compensation claim or retroactive pay raises under a contract. In each case it is necessary to determine the exact (or estimated) cost and which budget will have to bear the cost. Any action needed to reserve funds should then be taken concurrently with the actions terminating the employment. This action may not literally require the setting aside of money, but should at least consist of recording in the appropriate file the amount likely to be required from a contingency fund. It is particularly necessary that this be done in an institution where expenditures are departmentalized and there is no central fund available for emergency needs. Sometimes these subsequent expenditures may require that a position be held open for a period to generate enough savings, but this is, fortunately, not very common except in the case of restricted funds.

Most vacancies will be filled, and the same kind of planning is necessary for appointments. The decision on whether or not to fill a vacant position must, of course, come first and will be made within the general guidelines of the library and the institution. A position freeze or a policy of position review may impose arbitrary controls, and require rejustification. Alternatively either the budget rules or the union contracts may require certain procedures or preclude the possibility of reassignment. Although these decisions will naturally have a budgetary effect, the concern here is not with the politics but with the record needed. A replacement person will seldom receive exactly the same salary as the former incumbent. This situation arises from a variety of causes. Clerical scales, for example, usually provide for anniversary increments and may also provide for a learning period during which a reduced salary is paid. The implication is that the newcomer will receive a salary at or near the beginning of the range. There will, of course, be exceptions and one such is created by a lateral transfer when, since it is not usually institutional policy to reduce salaries, the new appointee may be transferred in at the existing salary level regardless of its relationship to the salary range. For faculty and other professional appointments, salaries are determined individually, according to qualifications, experience, etc., and may be subject to specific negotiation. Consequently one person's salary need bear no direct relation to the salary of another even in what is nominally the same position. It is true, however, that the influences of federal and union rules and regulations are tending to reduce the historic differentiations by academic rank and the part played by individual merit in arriving at a salary or a salary increment. Nevertheless more variability is still available for such appointments. In some institutions the differences have been formalized, resulting in increments over a preestablished base for specific qualifications and experience.

It is necessary first to determine the initial salary, and then to determine the date of appointment. It is at this stage that such matters as accrued leave on the part of the departing employee have an effect. Most institutions have guidelines as to permissible overlaps, usually allowing longer overlaps at higher levels of responsibility. Any overlap at all, of course, represents double payment for the same job during its continuance. This fact is not necessarily clear to supervisors when the terminated employee is not there, but has instead elected a lump-sum payment for unused vacation, but it is still a matter of double payment. Unless there is specific allowance made in the budget for such payments, or lapsed salaries are available, no overlap will be possible. This is a very bad management practice, but it is a common way of effecting economies. Other factors may also affect the appointment date. Where some or all of the salary is to be paid from grant money, or from the funds of another department, the date of availability for the grant or the financial needs of the other department may require actions not in line with the library's own requirements. Sometimes it is possible to negotiate a favorable change, but frequently the restriction must simply be accepted.

When both salary and time of appointment have been settled, there may remain some further internal accounting adjustments.

If the salary to be paid is less than that paid to the previous employee, and annual difference will become a permanent budget adjustment. Whether this goes to the library's discretionary funds or to those of the institution will depend on institutional policy. If the former is the case, it presents an opportunity to add to some other portion of the budget, either temporarily or permanently, but is must be remembered that for the year in question not all the savings will be available, because the salary for a portion of the year has already been paid at the higher rate to the ex-employee. If the new salary is higher, then the difference must be paid from some other source and represents a permanent decrease in that budget item, although in this case, for an appointment made at some time during a year, the full annual amount of the increase will not be paid. Understanding of these differentials is necessary for the proper exploitation of discretionary funds.

The other matter which most frequently causes misunderstanding is the handling of salary increases. This is simplest where the increments are known, as in a union contract, and where they occur either on anniversary dates or on the first day of a new fiscal year. Where, however, they are subject to individual negotiation or to institutional decisions that may differ each year, even the simple recording of the facts may become onerous, while the additon of federal and state concern with equal pay almost requires that the budget officer assume the role of watchdog. It is impossible to summarize neatly so complex a matter. Readers should be familiar with the various salary surveys published[4] that provide a general background and each budget officer should be familiar with the appropriate institutional policies. Rogers and Weber[5] give a brief but helpful survey of salary administration. The budget officer is responsible for seeing that institutional procedures are followed —for example, by ensuring that the proper payroll change form is processed at the right time and that the amounts are correct. It will also be a duty to check the entries on the budget payroll to ensure that they reflect changed salary rates. The budgetary role may become critical if the institution decides that part or all of the cost of salary increases must be offset by other decreases in the budget, whether by canceling vacant positions or by reductions in other kinds of expenditure. In such a case it is the responsibility of the budget officer to advise the library administration of the total cost of salary increases and of possible sources for necessary money.

Because academic salary increases are usually set in relation to fiscal years and many new appointments are made either late in the fiscal year or early in the next, it is necessary to have a fairly good idea of likely increases when recruiting. Policy on the payment of increases to new appointees varies widely, but it is generally a good idea to offer a new appointee in, say, April a salary comparable to that likely to be available for similar positions in July, and when creating new positions to set them up at a rate that incorporates likely salary increases for that range of positions or salaries.

Finally, accounts for nonregular or wage personnel require careful setting up. They must provide, as far as possible, for the wage needs of each department and must also allow for mandated increases in basic rates. Following the idealized distribution shown in Table 2, each department would be notified of the amount available for the year, and would be required to advise the personnel and budget offices of the persons on the wage payroll. In actual practice many names would carry forward each year, but each termination, appointment and rate increase should be reported as for regular, full-time personnel. As distinct from full-time salaries, the monthly totals for wages may differ substantially. It is to be expected that full-time employees will receive one-twelfth of their salaries each month and that in consequence the amount allowed in the budget will be spent out at a regular rate, affected only by prolonged vacancies or position freezes. Wage employees, however, frequently fill in gaps, or help to carry the library through peak-load periods. For this reason wage expenditures tend to follow the academic pattern of the institution. Consequently if summer activity is low, wage expenditures are likely, in the absence of special projects, to be low also. This kind of difference must be borne in mind when monitoring expenditures. When projecting annual expenditures, care must be taken to project at a monthly rate which reflects past experience and is appropriate to the period of the academic year remaining. (See Diagram 2.) For instance, if during the summer the monthly rate of expenditure is $12,000, but during the remaining nine months it is $24,000, a projection being made in December should reckon the expenditure through June at the latter rate rather than at the summer rate or any average of the two.

In order to provide figures in the form required for state, federal and other reports, it is necessary to distinguish between student and nonstudent employees both in money and in hours worked. The accounts should, therefore, enable the library to make this distinction. Local institutional conventions govern the recording of money and services received under such federal programs as work-study grants, but libraries must keep records of the number of students employed, the number of hours worked and the dollar amount of the aid so provided, since this knowledge is required for budgetary planning.

The objectives of monitoring personnel expenditures should be to determine how well they follow the original plan and to explain deviations where these occur.

LIBRARY MATERIALS

Because of their diversity, expenditures on library materials frequently prove hardest of all to monitor. The general objective is to spend the funds allotted as closely as possible in conformity with the library's plans. While the budget officer is seldom in charge of the ordering operation and may also have little to say on internal distribution, the responsibility remains, and must be exercised, of seeing that proper accounting procedures are used and that expenditures are properly authorized and correctly entered. The acquisitions librarian, or similar officer, must take responsibility for seeing that orders are placed and fulfiled and the appropriate invoices received and certified for payment. In turn the accountant, or other officer, must maintain records of their transmission to the institutional office charged with the disbursement of funds, and must verify the figures on the invoices. The library, in effect, vouches for the accuracy of the papers it forwards to the bursar or accountant, and this should be a controlling factor in any internal processes set up by the library. Books on acquisitions by Daniel Melcher[6] and Stephen Ford[7] cover many of the matters necessary in setting up a good control of expenditures on library materials. In addition the Bookdealer-Library Relations Committee of the Resources and Technical Services Division of the American Library Association has produced guidelines[8] that cover the handling of invoices and payments.

The progress of expenditures for materials should be checked at least monthly. Toward the end of the fiscal year this check should be carried out biweekly. At such times not only actual expenditures but encumbrances should be inspected, since the latter represent commitments to future expenditures. Encumbrances for book purchases present a very particular accounting problem because usually it is almost impossible to predict in advance the actual price that will be paid, which represents the result of an individual arithmetic exercise—published price of book, less discount, plus postage. Since in most cases only the first of these elements is known in advance, it is the usual practice to encumber book accounts at this value. Other methods have been proposed and used, such as standard unit costs, averaged discounts derived from historical records and the like, but none of them provide any greater final accuracy. If published price is used to encumber book purchases, in almost all instances the final payment will be less and it is therefore an equally common practice to overencumber to the likely equivalent of this difference. A range of 5 to 10 percent overencumbered has in the past been perfectly allowable. Increasing reliance on approval plans, and standing orders on the one hand, and reducing discounts, even the reverse, service charges, on the other, have made the practice an uncertain one. The best advice now appears to be to encumber at published price, liquidate this price at time of payment and debit the actual price paid. The accumulated record can then be used to determine how many further purchases are possible.

Approval plans, standing orders and all subscriptions are, in effect, preencumbrances. The very budget provisions for such purchases are based on expected expenditures. In such cases therefore the interest is in the achievement of the planned goals and in the under- or over-expenditure required to match reality with plan.

The pattern of publication during the year, the billing practices of serial suppliers, the effect of the academic year on the timing of orders and time-delays in the receipt of foreign publications are the four major external factors affecting the distribution of expenditures through the year. These must be taken into consideration when inspecting the accounts. It is, for example, usual for serial dealers to renew most subscriptions on a calendar-year basis and therefore to submit their major invoices to libraries some two to three months earlier to allow libraries time to make adjustments or claims. The result is usually a clustering of large payments around the end of the calendar year. For this reason concern at low expenditure rates is premature before this period, even though apparently large free balances are being carried forward by the library. Similarly expenditures on approval plans reflect the periods of heavier publication in fall and spring, which show up in a library's accounts a month or so later. Such variations will probably persist from year to year, and a comparison with last year's expenditures is more likely to reveal any serious perturbation than an estimate of proportionate expenditure for the current year.

It is, nevertheless, important to stress that orders for individual items should be placed as early as possible in the year, particularly for institutions unable to carry encumbered funds forward to the next year. So far as the author knows, there is no information available establishing either a normal curve of ordering, nor even outlining current practice, although studies undertaken by the Ohio College Library Center, by dealers and by processing centers may yet provide some useful background figures. Each institution should be aware of its own pattern or patterns and seek to correct any inefficiencies revealed. As a rough rule of thumb the budget should be encumbered (or spent), other than a reserve for urgent orders, and for standing orders, in the first nine or ten months of the fiscal year.

Some institutions have adopted an order year that runs two or three months before the fiscal year in order to match actual expenditures with the fiscal year. This is particularly appropriate when the proportion of foreign acquisitions is very high, delivery periods being longer for them than for domestic acquisitions. Use of this or any similar device depends on the institution's practice regarding encumbrances. Libraries that may not carry encumbrances forward, and must cancel outstanding orders, would benefit by using such a method. Where encumbrances, but not the funds, may be carried forward, the principal aim is not to have too great a sum carried forward in encumbrances because this interferes with the allocations for the next year, it being almost impossible to arrange that the encumbrances be proportional to the allocations. Where both the encumbrances and the funds encumbered may be carried forward, annual congruence becomes less important, though it is unusual for there to be no time limit within which the expenditures represented by those encumbrances must be made.

Wherever possible it is desirable that expenditures should bear a fairly close relationship to the proportion of the year that has elapsed. Where individual allocations are lagging behind, those responsible should be encouraged to increase their rate of ordering, while those ahead should be slowed down. Care must, however, be taken not to prevent essential expenditures nor to encourage spending for its own sake; and, in general, by the end of the third quarter, it should be understood that all unexpended funds are available for discretionary purchasing by the library.

During the year, the question arises of whether to attempt enforcement of a planned pattern of expenditure (*i.e.,* conformity to initial budget allocations) or to permit variations, based presumably on expressed need or even on evident ability to spend money. To some extent this dilemma can be resolved by requiring a certain level of expenditure to be reached at given times within the year. As was suggested, however, under the planning and setting up of a budget, individual allocations may best be regarded as planning guidelines rather than as strict controls. There is no simple answer. If the supply of money is tight, then overexpenditure by one area must clearly mean underexpenditure by another, unless ample reserves are available, which is unlikely to be the case in such a situation. In most cases a certain amount will have been reserved for special needs and this may be drawn on, where it can be demonstrated that the resulting benefits will be in line with the best interests of the library. In effect, control of expenditures for library materials requires a continuous conversation between budget officer, acquisitions officer and selector. Each of these, but particularly the first two, must be sensitive to real needs but also willing to draw the line when necessary. During the last two or three months of the fiscal year great care is needed in interpreting the reported figures, particularly those for encumbrances. Even when an allocation is overcommitted, examination of the encumbrances may indicate that a substantial proportion of these orders may possibly not come to charge. For example, foreign orders, or orders reported to be out-of-stock, may well have a delivery date beyond the end of the year. In that case, further local orders might well be placed, or the balance used for the purchase of desiderata, such as microforms, which can be obtained rapidly. None of these stratagems solves the basic question, which must be resolved within the philosophy of the library and according to the needs of the institution. If the basic plan was sound, then the goal should be to contain deviations within acceptable limits, recognizing that high expenditure in one year within an area may well be balanced by lower expenditure in another. For budgetary and political reasons it is, of course, highly desirable to spend all the money available in a year; it would be foolish to hold back on desirable purchases simply to comply with guidelines, however well conceived.

GOODS AND SERVICES

Generally speaking, most expenditures in this area are determined in advance. Such services as telephone, postage and rentals are billed at regular intervals and are therefore relatively easily monitored. Other categories such as supplies or travel are less regular, even though total expenditures may be predicted with some accuracy.

For relatively standard expenditures, it is a good practice to encumber annual estimated expenditures at the beginning of the year. A good example would be basic monthly telephone charges, which change only if rates increase or changes are made in the numbers and kinds of telephones. If this is done, the temptation to regard unspent funds as available for other purposes is reduced. Adjustments can easily be made if there are rate increases or decreases, while extra, variable charges for toll calls or the like can be recorded as the monthly billing is received.

Irregular expenditures present greater control problems, none more so than purchases of equipment. For the foreseeable future, inflation will render obsolete almost all price information available to a would-be purchaser, not because of any wilful concealment on the part of the vendor but because catalogs cannot be produced quickly enough to be up to date. In all such transactions, care must be taken to use initially the latest available information and to allow for price increases in estimating expenditure. A further complication, outside the control of any purchaser, is the time taken to deliver orders. Those with expertise in either the library or the institution can provide advice to assist in planning, but the best practice remains to order as early as possible within the fiscal year. The precaution of including on each order a specified delivery date with the alternative of cancellation will help to encourage prompt supply. In many institutions this practice is obligatory and no order can be carried past the end of a fiscal year. The order may be canceled and later revived, but such a procedure frequently confuses vendors. In any case a library that still requires undelivered equipment will have to be prepared to pay for it from the next year's funds. That leaves the disposition of the previously encumbered funds up for decision, and, if substantial, they are unlikely to be spent easily in the closing days of a fiscal year.

If by reason of nonsupply of orders, or unexpected extra funds, money is unspent towards the end of the year, consideration should be given to stockpiling essential supplies, such as paper, or paying advances on rentals or service contracts. Some institutions forbid the latter practice. This approach is the same as that which forbids prepayment for goods, even when substantial discounts may be obtained. It is understandable that an institution should object to being committed to uncertain purchases, but when the expenditure would be made anyway, the only justification available is that payments made within a year should refer to goods or services purchased within the same year. Admittedly, this is frequently mandated by state agencies and therefore cannot be circumvented. A further possibility is transfer of the balance between categories—for example, to library materials—but this, too, may be prohibited.[9]

Mostly the problem is not one of underexpenditure but one of undersupply of money. To forestall the situation in which essential payments cannot be made for lack of funds, expenditures should be checked monthly. Year-round charges should accrue at roughly 8 percent a month. Deviations should be noted and investigated. In some cases, however, the billing schedule may run behind the calendar early in the year, but be compressed at the end. Similarly, in some categories, historical circumstances may place major expenditures at certain times of the year. For example, orders for annual supplies of cards for circulation or cataloging may be sent out on bid in September, the information enabling a firm order to be placed may be received in October, and the cards themselves received and paid for in Janaury. It would be necessary to keep this situation in mind when deciding on other possibilities for the purchase of supplies at the beginning of the year.

The procedures by which materials (other than library materials) must be ordered are usually determined for the institution as a whole and centrally controlled. This reduces the flexibility available to any one unit within the institution and may become the one determining factor in deciding how to spend either accumulated surpluses or specially allocated funds received late in the fiscal year. It is usually easier to buy library materials than to face the numerous reviews, such as bidding requirements, that accompany orders for equipment or renovations. Nevertheless, the administrator must be guided by the needs of the library. Such an occasion may, for example, be the only time in the next few years when microfilm readers can be bought to replace existing ones, and the chance should be made good.

External conditions may also offer the library the chance to improve its financial standing. It may be possible to purchase equipment which is presently either leased or rented. Generally a rental arrangement allows for replacement by more up-to-date equipment. For this reason rental is very common with computers. It may, however, be the case that the equipment in question, a photocopier for example, is performing adequately, has a very low incidence of maintenance, and is likely to meet the library's needs for a long period of time. Usually there is not available sufficient money to pay for conversion of lease to purchase, but if year-end funds are available, purchase now would reduce the rental costs for the next and subsequent years. All other things being equal, the decision to purchase would be fiscally sound. Other instances will suggest themselves to the reader. The elements to be considered in each case are the long-term fiscal effects, the ability of the budget to absorb a one-time expenditure and the desirability of the purchase in relation to the library's program. The bringing of such matters to the attention of the administration is one of the principal goals of any monitoring activity.

INCOME

So far the discussion has been concerned solely with expenditures, but it would not be proper to conclude this chapter without a short glance at special sources of income. Unless there are substantial endowments or a major gift-giving program, a very high proportion of any library's income is determined at the beginning of the year. Moreover, libraries are not usually income-producing units. There are, however, some standard sources of income, such as fines, photoduplication charges and sale of publications. In the absence of major program changes, the amount of income from these sources should remain fairly stable. It must be recognized, of course, that the income is offset by expenditures incurred in its production. Generally speaking, this will balance the income, since the library's motive in charging fines, for example, is not profit.

In some situations, however, the relationship of income and expenditure is not so clear. A library may decide, perhaps in order to reduce administrative costs, to farm out certain activities. A contract for the provision of photoduplication services via the use of coin-operated machines will transfer from the library's own photoduplication office a volume of routine activity, allowing the office to concentrate on more specialized activities and on the library's own internal needs. In such a contract provision may well be made for payment of rent, either as fixed payments or as a percentage of total income. The first would be constant, though open to renegotiation each year, but the second would be variable and subject to adjustment during the year, while in each case consideration would have to be given to effects on the library's own operations.

A second kind of variable concerns the sale of library materials or equipment or the reimbursement of the library by another unit for services rendered. The disposition of materials owned by an institution may be governed by quite rigorous procedures but the instrumentalities set up to carry out these procedures are generally inadequate to meet the needs of a library in disposing of library materials, whether withdrawn, duplicates or received by gift. In some instances the control exercised is so extreme that the only means available for disposition are destruction and exchange for value. Where, however, the library is permitted to dispose of surplus materials, the income derived may not even then be solely at the disposition of the library. Transactions within the one fiscal year are not generally questioned, though it is usually necessary to specify the type of transaction—*e.g.*, sale of duplicates, refund of double payment, cancellation of subscription. Where, however, more than one fiscal year is involved and the amount is substantial, the accountant will point out, and correctly, that the proper procedure is to relate that income to a surplus and deficiency account for the year when the original transaction took place. The result, of course, is that the money goes to a general contingency fund and, while the library may draw on that fund, the income is in effect lost. Even when direct sales are allowed to be counted as income, the problem remains of where the income should be applied. Since the initial budget was set up including an advance estimate of income, no adjustment can be made until that income has been exceeded. If, however, any particular sale is of a special nature and unlikely to have been included in the original estimate of sales income, then it is permissible by temporary budget amendment to increase both income and expenditure. The expenditure assignment may be made in the category and allocation area that generated the income, though care must be taken to guard against having such funds accrue always to favored areas when others, to which such sales are inaccessible, are languishing for lack of funds. In other words the general good must come before the specific good.

Special circumstances may arise when the library receives credit notes rather than cash payments. It is a common practice to consolidate all receipts and payments in one vendor account in the central accounting office. In such a situation credit notes become common property, which may affect the library's expenditure records, but which may have a much more drastic sideeffect if, for example, payments for subscriptions are not processed but held against outstanding credit notes. In such circumstances it is desirable that the library's accounts should be separated from those of bookstores or other academic units. At the least, if that cannot be done, some system of perferential treatment for essential payments such as subscription renewals should be devised.

THE REPORTING FUNCTION

During the year the progress in expenditures should be reported on regularly. These reports need not be elaborate nor need they always cover the total budget, but they must be reliable and presented in an understandable format:

> Reports to administrative officers and governing boards furnish current information concerning the operations of the institution without which intelligent administration is impossible.[10]

These reports need to be made to those responsible for making decisions. The chief acquisitions librarian, for example, needs to know how much money has been spent and how much has been encumbered. In turn, this information needs to be broken down by fund and the information passed on the selectors and others responsible individually for those funds. Those who receive financial reports should be prepared to examine them analytically, since their principal use is "the comparison and reporting of actual performance against approved plans or programs,"[11] an essential element of control. The reason for deviations should be examined carefully and corrective action taken. Such action may range from the correction of an error in the accounts to a major shift of funds rendered necessary by unforeseen needs. Such changes are not of their nature bad. Academia is, in itself, unpredictable and care must be taken not to preclude a necessary response to change by rigid insistence on a specific breakdown of expenditures. The goals of any monitoring operation must be to ensure that the budget is responsive to institutional need.

NOTES

1. *College and University Business Administration* (1973), p. 162.
2. Rogers and Weber (1971), p. 103.
3. *Ibid.*, p. 102.
4. Association of Research Libraries, *Salary Survey* published annually. Each year the *Library Journal* publishes an article reviewing librarians' salaries.
5. Rogers and Weber (1971), pp. 40–43.
6. Melcher (1971), especially the chapters: "Encumbering—Master or Servant," pp. 38–45; "The Fallacy of the Bid Process," pp. 46–55; and "The Going Discounts," pp. 56–72.
7. Ford (1973).
8. American Library Association (1973), especially Section VI, "Financial Requirements."
9. Robins (1973), pp. 51–52. This short discussion, in layman's language, explains the causes, needs and constraints of budget amendments during the year.
10. Scheps and Davidson (1970), p. 356.
11. Williams (1970), p. 50.

Chapter 12

Closing out the Budget

> *It is perfectly reasonable to expect a library to live with the funds made available to it.*
> (Barnes, 1971.)

Institutions of higher education are not under the pressure of the marketplace to align income and expenditure in the production of goods that must be priced to sell at a profit. "This weak tie between income and expenditure" leads to the kind of administrative separation that makes the efficient allocation of funds difficult to achieve.[1] For cost effectivenss and the profit motive, educational institutions subsitute the achievement of goals and objectives. The original budget as conceived by the institution was designed to further these goals. No matter how careful the administration is, toward the end of the each year discrepancies of various kinds will almost certainly have emerged. The action taken to counteract these tendencies depends on the degree of flexibility available to the institution. Where transfer between categories of expenditure or programs is permitted, unused funds may be so transferred rather than wasted. Whether this is done by actual budget transfer or by the balancing of over- and under-expenditures is immaterial to the individual fund administrator, who will be more concerned to make effective use of the funds thus provided.

It is at this period of the year that administrators are apt to ask librarians whether they can spend a few more thousand dollars on books. Librarians seldom turn down such an offer, but accepting it can frequently cause serious logistical problems. It is seldom understood by the administrator that his kindness just may be act of irresponsibility. As Barnes describes it, the requirement that a library live within its budget is acceptable, but problems arise when the librarian "is not given clear policy directions other than those associated with financial limitations."[2] As indicated in another context by Summers,[3] this kind of lump-sum charity indicates not concern for library needs, but rather the opposite, a careless unconcern with the need for planning. Librarians have, however, learned to live with such an attitude, and by doing so have incorporated it into their planning; hence, the standard practice of maintaining wishing-lists of expensive items.

The goal of the individual administrator is to spend the money assigned to the unit as closely as possible in accordance with the plans of that unit. Libraries, quite apart from year-end bonuses, also face discrepancies arising from changed plans, nondeliveries of purchases and the like. In closing out the budget, the administrator will be concerned to use this leftover money as effectively as possible. How this is accomplished will depend first on the time when the information becomes available, second on the flexibility allowed and third on the kinds of discrepancies revealed by budget reports. Ideally, the knowledge of unexpended funds should not be received so late that there is nothing to be done. Occasionally, however, an unexpected resignation or failure to deliver an expensive piece of equipment will leave a considerable balance in hand with little lead time for planning.

All budgeting should contain contingency plans, whether or not they are worked out in detail. As the year advances and achievements are measured against goals, certain kinds of remedial actions will make themselves either evident or necessary. There is seldom an acquisitions program unable to purchase collections or back-runs of periodicals. Or there may be the opportunity for a year-end project such as the shifting around of collections, or the repainting and renovation of a reading room. The marshalling and costing-out of such projects, which are then held in reserve, greatly simplifies the rapid reallocation of resources. Forward purchase of supplies in common use is also a standard and perfectly defensible practice. It is not, however, usually possible to pay in advance for services or goods to be supplied in the next fiscal period, although an exception will sometimes be made for purchases that, like periodical subscriptions, are continuous in nature, particularly when forward payment brings with it a satisfactory discount.

The most common problem is estimating what proportion of outstanding orders for library materials will come to charge. Because of this uncertainty, most libraries either overencumber or work on the basis of an order year that begins and ends earlier than the fiscal year. The importance and the timing of this problem depends on whether the institution follows an accrual or a cash basis of accounting. A further response is possible, if allowed by the institution. Whereas most state or general funds must be expended within the fiscal year, the same rule frequently does not apply to special or endowment funds, which normally continue from year to year. If expenditures have been made on these funds for purchases that might equally well have ben made on general funds, then a portion of that expenditure might well be transferred to general funds. The reverse transaction is of course equally possible. Whether it can be done or not will depend both on the institution's rules for accounting and the compatibility of such a transfer with the rules governing expenditure from the special fund. The need, for example, to report specific purchases or to use special book plates would make the maneuver impossible. If the transfer can be made, it has the double effect of painlessly drawing down an otherwise useless balance in general funds and of restoring to use next year an equivalent amount of money in the special fund. Care would, of course, need to be taken not to diminish expenditures that are required as matching funds for a grant or as maintenance-of-effort for federal funding.

Most institutions have a set timetable for the actual closing of the books of account. These instructions must be studied carefully and adhered to. It is usual, for example, for the closing date for the receipt of foreign invoices to precede that for domestic ones, because, for the foreign, the processing of the resulting checks through the banking system and the allocation of bank charges takes longer. Yet it may be that where conversions into U.S. dollars have already been made on the these invoices, they will be accepted after other foreign invoices are being held. Equally, payments to overseas vendors, which may be paid to an address in the U.S., count as domestic payments. This kind of regulation requires thorough understanding on the part of all those concerned with the processing of invoices within the library. One other monetary control that may become of critical importance at the end of the year is the manner in which the institution handles credit notes. If these are placed in a common account it is possible that invoices processed by the library for payment may be held up beyond the end of the fiscal year. A regular routine should be set up to check whether this is so. As a footnote to this kind of situation, libraries are well advised to hold to a minimum any miscellaneous income at the end of each year.

Different cut-off dates may also be set for various categories of expenditure. Wage payments, which may take longer to process because the amounts are not known in advance, may well be cut off before the end of the year since otherwise the actual checks could not be written before the last acceptable day. Equipment, for audit reasons, may be paid for only if actually received before the end of the fiscal year, even though the invoice itself may not be processed until later, during the customary period of grace. It is not usual for invoices dated after the end of the fiscal year to be accepted for payment (other than in the accrual situation) unless they clearly refer to goods ordered and received during the fiscal year, and then only during any period while the accounts are in the process of being closed. This period, usually referred to as the period of grace, is mostly short, perhaps a week, and is allowed because the paper work required in closing the books is too massive within a large institution for it to be practicable to shift overnight from one fiscal year to the next. It is necessary to remember, however, that at the same time the institution will be setting up the next year's accounts and directing some payments toward that year too, while holding or forbidding other kinds of payments and budget adjustments. During this period there is little flexibility and very little chance for the exercise of discretion. Once time has run out the library must live with the results of the year's work.

At this stage the one remaining activity of the fiscal year is the compilation of a final budget report, while at the same time preparing for the next year, which has, after all, already begun. "Educational institutions function as owners, operators and trustees"[4] and need to report accordingly. These functions are reflected in the reports to the units, variably according to the emphasis of the unit concerned. The report is required to show what has been done with the money made available during the year, namely what assets have been acquired and what services have been performed. Whatever reports are prepared,

> Their main function is to call attention to major discrepancies where actual performance is considerably different from the budget estimate.[5]

This does not imply failure or perversity on the part of the unit or of any individual, but rather the unpredictability of any major activity. Inflation in, say, Germany, may have been greater than expected and the expenditures on books will reflect this fact. Federal requirements may have raised wage expenditures beyond the capacity of the planned contingency fund. Any of a hundred other things may have happened. It is necessary to know what these factors were, how they were coped with and what effect they finally had on plans and expenditures. As Dougherty and Heinritz put it, "every administrator should be able to determine the cost of his library."[6] This determination can only be made by keeping and using adequate records of expenditure. Without this knowledge the ability to plan for the next and succeeding years is hampered. (See Table 15.)

The initial analysis can be relatively simple, consisting mostly of totals for each category of expenditure, which show gross differences from the initial planned expenditures in those categories. Such information can expedite the initial setting up of allocations for the next year. More detail is, however, required if the analysis is to show how nearly the library achieved its goals. As suggested by

Williams, "such analyses, both qualitative and quantitative, should be concerned with the relationships between expenditures and results."[7]

This critical examination is particularly important for the planning of any acquisition program for library materials where a great

Table 15. Projected and Actual Expenditures for the Fiscal Year 197–

	Budget	Actual
Personnel-Related Expenses		
Full-time positions	1,755,000	1,712,000
Wages	235,000	280,000
Allotment		
Goods and services	200,000	237,000
Library materials	950,000	1,001,000
Reserve	60,000	6,000*
Total	$3,200,000	$3,236,000
Income	$45,000	$51,000

*Balance unused at end of fiscal year. The remainder was transferred as shown in Table 13.

Comments: The increase in total expenditure reflects increased income for the year and a special grant for the purchase of equipment. Personnel-related expenses reflect the combination of permanent adjustments made (outlined in Table 13) and unexpended salaries resulting from vacancies. A high proportion of the latter was transferred to wages to provide temporary assistance. Goods and Services expenditures reflect transfers from Reserve to cover increased costs.

Library Materials expenditures reflect transfers from salary savings for special purchases.

variety of factors may have caused major and minor changes during the year, some of which, such as cost increases for periodicals, may continue into the future, while another, such as the purchase of a costly special collection, may not recur or, if it does, probably in a different subject field. Since the original objective of allocations by subject or by academic unit was to match acquisition money against perceived needs, it is important to be able to estimate how effectively those needs were estimated and met. If they were met, adjustments in future allocations will be less than if there were severe over- and under-achievements.

A second set of information derived from this analysis will concern efficiency, namely, how well the routines of ordering and purchasing were carried out. This can be derived from the amounts still encumbered at the end of the year and by the estimation of unpaid bills as compared with those on hand at a similar time last year. It is, of course, essential to know what encumbrances are carried forward, particularly if they are simply a first call on the new year's money, but their existence may be used to encourage better purchasing patterns. If they are too large they may distort the new allocations and it may be necessary to cancel some of the outstanding orders. This kind of information provides an essential management tool.

Equally important is the information provided by an analysis of expenditures on goods and services, since this provides the latest in facts on which to base estimates for the new year. Variations in these areas are generally those caused by rising prices and may also reflect the secondary effects of purchases, as when new equipment requires an increases in the payments for maintenance; but attention must be paid to the effects of one-time expenditures. A major renovation this year may, for example, need to be followed up next year with the purchase of equipment or the costs of transferring books and other materials. Projected purchases that could not be completed should also be highlighted in order to determine whether a further attempt should be made. Similarly, half-completed projects should be noted, since it will be necessary to complete them or regard past expenditures as wasted. These observations are of the nature of warning flags, letting the budget-maker know what to be aware of and what to plan for.

This activity may accompany or be performed as an internal audit, which relates the control of spending to the accomplishment of its objectives. It will, in any case, be beneficial as work preparatory to any other audit conducted by or for the institution. It should include a review of internal control policies and how well they have functioned, the verification of inventory and other property listing such as statistics on library materials and the examination of all special accounts in order to be able to respond to questions asked by other auditors.[8]

Finally, it is expected that the chief administrator will prepare in summary form an annual report, part of which must be concerned with finance, and information concerning expenditures will enable appropriate comments to be made whether concerning achievements or needs. To this report, fiscal reports form proper appendices and provide the information needed to answer the innumerable questionnares that seem ever poised to descend on any administrator. At this stage the budget cycle is complete and another one has begun, benefiting, it is hoped, from the lessons learned in the course of the year.

NOTES

1. Williams (1970), p. 11. Chapter 2, "The Problem of University Budgeting," is a useful and succinct summary of the differences from business which make the analysis and planning of university budgets so difficult both to achieve and to understand.
2. Barnes (1971), p. 102.
3. Summers, p. 1175.
4. *College and University Business Administration* (1968), p. 165.
5. Robins (1973), p. 52.
6. Dougherty and Heinritz (1966), p. 150.
7. Williams (1970), p. 12.
8. *College and University Business Administration* (1968). Chapter 21, "Internal Control and Audits," gives a good general background on the need for and ways of auditing.

Chapter 13

Retrospect: Important Issues to Remember

> *It is recognized that politics are never excluded from any system. However, the deliberations can be carried out more effectively with pertinent information than if they are undertaken in a vacuum.* (Parden, 1970.)

Budgetary control is a major element in management, a tool that assists administration in analysis and decision-making. Even though libraries in an academic institution are not set up to make a profit, they must operate both effectively and efficiently. In the absence of a marketplace mechanism, the library "must substitute analytical studies of its activities and their direction and level."[1] These studies, while they will use other measures and other sources of information, must ultimately be translated into financial plans. The budget is the document that expresses these plans. It provides, in Parden's words, "visibility to the decisions affecting the allocation of resources."[2] This visibility encourages commitment to achieve the goals represented by that allocation. Not everyone recognizes the situation referred to by Barnes "that resources are limited and wants are unlimited"[3] and the greater the knowledge of and the participation in the budget process of those responsible for expenditures the greater is the hope that they will understand the limitations imposed by finite resources and the need for choice between alternatives that this implies. Whether or not this optimism is justified, it is certainly easier to work with people who are not overawed by the mystique that frequently surrounds the budget process.

The word "process" is an important one to understand. Budgets and budgetary control are dynamic, not static, things. There is a certain inexorability about financial planning.

> The compilation of the annual budget is an automatic due date requiring that the long-range plan for the next year be ready to translate into an operating budget.[4]

The aim of any administrator should be to mitigate this inexorability by good forward planning, particularly in libraries where activities are continuous, without the discontinuities imposed by a term system. It is simply not possible to stop library processes without paying a heavy price in disorganization. A library in effect depends on patterns of activity and is therefore both peculiarly resistant to change and peculiarly fragile in the face of drastic change. These facts must be recognized in fiscal management.

Recent years have introduced several elements of change. Internally the advent of computerization has offered, for a price, a way to reduce some of the labor intensivity characteristic of libraries. In itself such a possibility is traumatic enough for a conservative profession, but to it has been added the significant downward shift in both public and private support of higher education. This shift has meant sharper competition for available dollars and the fact that the machine, once installed, must, as it were, be fed is not always palatable even in the face of strong arguments concerning reduced unit costs in the future.[5] At the other end of the spectrum fewer dollars are available for the library's traditional mainstay, the book, and newer media such as data bases are nibbling away on the fringes. Changes of this magnitude require careful rethinking and restructuring of budgets. Schmidt predicts correctly that "the formulae and matrices devised during the period of growth and grandeur will be of small comfort and little use for the problems ahead."[6] This note, though negative, is not pessimistic. It is rather a challenge to librarians to make effective use of such tools as budgetary control to analyze their activities and to develop the necessary new ways of seeing.[7]

Accountability is a theme running through much recent writing, and libraries are not immune. According to Mortimer, "There will be great pressure to relate efficiency to educational effectivness."[8] Such pressures require that librarians demonstrate when necessary that the appearance of inefficiency—*e.g.,* in the staffing of public service desks—actually leads to greater effectiveness in terms of user satisfaction. To achieve this end, librarians need to develop more sophistication in the development and use of statistics and make wider use of cost studies and analytical models. They need also to develop more skill in exploring alternative programs for the use of limited resources.

As a profession, librarians have been slow to use the ungentlemanly tools of the accountant and the analyst. The many studies now appearing indicate that this attitude is passing from the library scene. Libraries are complex organizations, with somewhat diffuse goals, where quality and quantity intermingle. They need careful nurture if their growth is to be orderly and self-sustaining. Among the many skills needed to provide this nurture are those of the budgetary expert alongside those of the expert reference librarian and the antiquarian bookman. These skills must go hand in hand, since the one must respond to the other. Such a response can only be called forth by the mutual sharing of expertise, which is the true objective of·the development and handling of budgets.

NOTES
1. Williams (1970), p. 12.
2. Parden (1970), p. 53.
3. Barnes (1971), p. 96.
4. Parden (1970), p. 52.
5. Baumol and Marcus (1973), p. 44 ff.
6. Schmidt, "Resource Allocation in University Libraries," p. 647.
7. During the writing of this book, it was announced that William Kurth had received a Council on Library Resources Grant to explore the development of a model audit for university libraries. From research such as this will be derived the new models which libraries will need to help them cope with change.
8. Mortimer (1972), p. 48.

APPENDIX

The State University Libraries: a Case Study

In order to free budgetary projections from the bias inherent in examining an actual library system, an imaginary library "The State University Libraries" was set up as a model on which to test the effects of various budgetary constraints. A five-year history was constructed and references in the text are to this history. The State University Libraries are oganized in much the same way as most medium and large university libraries. They also face the same problems in intra institutional relations and the same budgetary problems. A case study of our imaginary library is appended in the hope that it will stimulate others to prepare case histories in which budget problems can be studied.

 The State University is a medium-large institution with 20,000 students, 2,500 faculty and professional staff and 2,000 other employees. It enjoys an average reputation with two or three of the thirty-six graduate programs verging on excellence. Over the years Agriculture, Engineering and the Physical Sciences have been the mainstay of the academic program. The Liberal Arts and Humanities had always been second-class citizens, but the last ten years have seen considerable growth in these areas, growth which unfortunately for them came just at the end of the years of strong financial support.

 To meet the demands of this institution the libraries have a total budget of $3,200,000, which is approximately 4 percent of the total institutional budget. The budget has grown dramatically over the past five years and, while the most visible evidence is the library materials budget, which has increased from $301,000 to $950,000, the increase in personnel-related expenditures is even more dramatic. Five years ago there were only 50 full-time positions. There are now 172. Whereas previously salaries were uncompetitive nationally, even regionally, the libraries are now able to recruit the best talent. The budget figure has risen in five years from $850,000 to $1,990,000. While these sets of figures include and are therefore reduced by allowances for inflation, the university administration has clearly been aware of and willing to supply the needs of the libraries. The libraries are in a fairly strong positon for this reason and wish to maintain it. In any period of fiscal trouble, the goal is to maintain the general shape of the libraries in order to take adequate advantage of any spare funds the administration can find.

The State University Libraries:
Initial Budget Statement.

Personnel Related:	Full-time positions (172)	1,755,000	
	Wages	235,000	1,990,000
Goods and Services:	Supplies	40,000	
	Communications	20,000	
	Maintenance	20,000	
	Repairs and Renovations	15,000	
	Rentals	25,000	
	Computer Services	30,000	
	Miscellaneous	10,000	
	Travel and Research Support	15,000	
	Equipment	25,000	200,000
Library Materials:	Books	400,000	
	Periodicals	500,000	
	Binding	50,000	950,000
Contingency Fund			60,000
TOTAL			$3,200,000
Library Income (included in above)			$45,000

A short general description of the libraries will provide a background for the financial history which follows. Most of the detailed budget distributions appear in the text. For that reason, only abbreviated tables are used in this description.

The expansion, evident here as in other libraries during the sixties, has slowed down. Quite apart from the reductions caused by inflation, the lack of space and the slower academic growth of the university have caused a reassessment of collection growth. The most optimistic growth projection is now 4 to 5 percent per year. Title II funds and special supplements were principally to build up microforms and other special collections. Such activities have now been greatly reduced, but they have left behind them a serious legacy of processing and cataloging problems.

Personnel Distribution.
(For more detail see Table 2.)

Department	No. of Professionals	No. of Semiprofessionals	No. of Clerks	FTE* Wages	Total Cost
Administration	5	2	8	2.5	$ 184,000
Acquisitions	4	3	8	3.5	162,000
Cataloging	12	4	20	4.5	400,000
Serials	3	3	15	6.0	210,000
General Services	5	3	8	7.0	194,000
Lending Services	2	2	14	8.0	199,000
Reference Services	10	3	8	6.0	269,000
Reserve Services	2	1	5	6.0	89,000
Special Collections	2	1	2	2.0	75,000
Science	2	1	3	2.5	75,000
Engineering	1	1	2	2.0	51,000
Life Sciences	2	1	3	2.5	72,000
TOTALS	50	26	96	52.5	$1,990,000

*FTE for wages implies 2,000 hours per year at a basic rate of $2.00 per hour; divergences from this basic equivalent result from the payment of higher hourly rates in some instances.

APPENDIX *The State University Libraries: a Case Study* / **181**

    The public services staff is lively and keen to help readers, hence the high numbers of reference questions. The very high number of directional-ready information questions, some 100,000 a year, is balanced by 20,000 intenseive research questions. About a dozen classes are given some library instruction each term and 25 to 30 small groups received counseling in term-paper preparation.

    The picture is that of a relatively healthy library, in sufficiently good shape to withstand pressures, whether budgetary or programmatic, for at least a while. It has not, however, given more than passing consideration to technological change and this tokenism could become a major problem, if external conditions change. Against this background, the events of five years will be postulated, reacting to a varying fiscal direction for the university. There is no claim that each decision is the best that could be made but it is instructive to explore other decisions and to realize that very narrow range of alternatives available.

Library Materials Distribution.

Area	Books	Periodicals	Binding	Total
Arts and Performing Arts [1]	$25,000	$25,000	$3,000	$53,000
Humanities	50,000	60,000	6,000	116,000
Social Sciences [2]	50,000	65,000	6,000	121,000
Languages	40,000	45,000	5,000	90,000
Education	10,000	10,000	1,000	21,000
Sciences	25,000	90,000	9,000	124,000
Engineering	20,000	55,000	5,000	80,000
Life Sciences	20,000	70,000	6,500	96,500
Reference	15,000	35,000	5,000	55,000
General [3]	100,000	40,500	3,000	143,000
Reserves	20,000	500	-	20,000
Special Collections	25,000	4,000	500	29,500
	$400,000	$500,000	$50,000	$950,000

Notes: [1] Includes small Art History Program
      [2] Includes Psychology, Documents, Law
      [3] Includes Browsing Collection, small blanket orders, microforms (both sets and subscriptions), newspapers and areas of general interest to all.

Definitions of Departments at the State University Libraries.

Departments

Administration

Acquisitions

Cataloging

Serials

General Services

Lending Services

Reference Services

Reserve Services

Special Collections

Branch Libraries
Science

Engineering

Life Sciences

Definitions

Includes top administrators (3), Accounts, Personnel, Budget, Mailroom, Maintenance.

Includes preorder searching, gifts and exchange and assistance to Bibliographers.

Includes all catalog maintenance (filing, revising, etc.).

Includes cataloging, periodicals room, and binding.

Includes Quick Reference, Information, Browsing Room, Instruction, Microforms.

Includes circulation, stack maintenance, Interlibrary Loan, Photoduplication.

Includes three Bibliographer/Subject Specialists and Documents.

Includes both Graduate and Undergraduate Reserves and provides study help to students or classes.

Includes a Rare Book Room, some archives, and a special collection with a small endowment. Both Professionals are subject specialists.

Covers Chemistry, Physics, Mathematics.

Covers Engineering including Bio-engineering, Technology.

Covers Biology, Zoology, Health Sciences, Agriculture.

APPENDIX *The State University Libraries: a Case Study* / **183**

Other Information.

Size of collection		900,000 cataloged volumes
		250,000 documents
		50,000 maps
		520,000 microforms
		50,000 uncataloged volumes
Hours open per week		100
Age of main library building		15 years
Time left for expansion of collections		3 years
Activity indicators:		
Number of library users		900,000
Collection Usage:		
Circulated	200,000	
In-house	550,000	
Reserves	250,000	1,000,000
Reference Services		250,000
Interlibrary Loan (includes photo-duplication)		50,000
Collection Growth:		
Number of books added	30,000	
Associated activities	60,000	
Number of serial parts added	150,000	
Associated activities	50,000	
Number of other materials added	200,000	
Associated activities	100,000	590,000
Catalog maintenance (Number of cards)		550,000

Budgetary Action: First Year

The University has guaranteed a 10 percent salary increase and has also allowed a 5 percent in the base budget, with no limitation on where the sum should be applied, provided that the distribution proposed is properly justified. In case terms this means:

Total Salary Increase	$199,000
Base Budget Increase	160,000

The library administration has to consider requests for new support and examine what actual changes must be considered.

The requests are:

(1) Faculty in the program want an Asian specialist, but the program is very small.

(2) Technical Operations wants another cataloger to help with the "backlog".

(3) Students want longer hours of opening.

(4) Several areas in the library support requests for new database services and more instruction.

The background data are:

(1) Book prices have risen 5 percent; periodical prices have risen 15 percent; binding costs are steady; prices for supplies and similar items have risen 5 percent.

(2) Student enrollment will go up by 1,000.

(3) The university has instituted a new graduate program in Business, by expanding Accounting and combining it with Economics. The initial enrollment is expected to be 75 students.

(4) Five new catalog cabinets are needed.

(5) Circulation has risen by 20,000.

(6) Reserve usage has risen by 50,000.

(7) Reference questions have remained the same.

What must be done to maintain existing programs at approximately the same level?

To maintain the same buying program will require:

Books	$20,000	
Periodicals	75,000	$95,000

Increased costs for supplies will account for   5,000
To maintain the circulation staff/work ration requires:

	Clerk	$ 7,000	
	Wages	5,000	12,000

To maintain the reserve staff/work ratio requires:

	Clerk	$8,000	
	Wages	5,000	13,000

These unavoidable increases, which simply maintain the existing program will require a total of $125,000

The announced new program requires added resources and staff:

	Books	$10,000	
	Periodicals	5,000	
	Binding	500	15,500
	Librarian	15,000	15,000
	TOTAL		$30,500

The balance of the $160,000 made available must then be used to reduce the impact of inflation in other areas of Goods and Services $4,500

The result of these budget decisions can be shown thus:

	Base Budget	*1st Year Budget Request*
Personnel	$1,990,000	$2,224,000
Library Materials	950,000	1,060,500
Goods and Services	200,000	209,500
Reserve	60,000	60,000
TOTAL	$3,200,000	$3,559,000

Despite a dollar increase of $359,000 in the total budget, the changes have been minimal. Full-time staff has increased from 172 to 175, and there has been an FTE increase of 2 in wage help. Library materials have been increased only by the amount purchased for the new program, about 1,000 books and 250 new serials.

Because the increase for goods and services was minimal, savings generated from vacant positions and borrowing from the reserve fund will be used to purchase the five catalog cabinets and to renovate the main catalog area, which is long overdue for such attention. Other salary savings will be used to provide part-time help for cataloging.

There was no way to provide for increased hours, though some adjustments were made by reducing hours open during term-breaks and providing longer hours during examination periods.

Budgetary Action: Second Year

Inflation continues to increase and the appropriations received by the university are not keeping pace. A university-wide cut of 3 percent is announced, the returns from which will be used in part to meet the standing commitment to a 10 percent salary increase. For the library, this particular gift-horse will now cost $106,770, about two-thirds of the increase received in the preceding year.

At this stage the signals received by the library administration become wildly contradictory:

(1) The faculty still wants an Asian specialist.

(2) The students still want longer hours.

(3) The university administration expects greater productivity.

(4) Cataloging arrearages have grown. The cost per unit cataloged is now so high that automation appears the only way out.

(5) Circulation figures have remained stable, but in-library use has risen by 50 percent. An inventory during the summer has, however, revealed a disturbingly high loss rate.

(6) Reshelving of the collections on two whole floors is necessary because of uneven (and changing) expansion rates within the collections. This is rendered doubly awkward because the area in

question contains a high proportion of outsize shelving and any move will change service patterns.

(7) The microform area has shown a 25 percent increase in use and more readers are required.

(8) Book prices have increased 10 percent; periodical price increases range from 10 to 20 percent. The binding contract includes a 5 percent price increase.

Representations based on these facts persuade the university administration to reduce the library's share of the budget cut to 2 percent or $71,180, on the understanding that as far as possible the cut will be applied to personnel.

There are six vacant positions:
        One professional cataloger
        One reference librarian
        Two clerks in lending services
        One clerk in serials
        One semiprofessional in general services.

The library administration has now to meet the external demands placed on them by the university in the form of a budget cut and the internal demands relating to inertia and pressure for services. Two areas, Acquisitions and cataloging and Lending services will be examined in depth, and the remaining analysis presented in outline only.

(1) *Acquisitions and cataloging.*

(a) *Library materials.* No university money is available to meet the costs of inflation and internal reallocation possibilities are likely to be small. It is therefore certain that the present buying program will be curtailed. To keep pace with inflation the following increases would be needed:

Category	Inflation Rate	Year-One Budget	Increase
Books	10%	$430,000	$43,000
Periodicals	15% (av.)	580,000	87,000
Binding	5%	50,500	2,525
		$1,060,500	$132,525

Clearly such an amount cannot be found from other areas of the library budget. The maintenance of all subscriptions alone would require $89,525 (with binding). If no other adjustment were made to the total budget for library materials, books would effectively suffer a 20 percent decrease. Despite faculty and library resistance, it is decided that $20,000 worth of subscriptions, marginal or duplicate, must be canceled. Limits will be placed on the numbers of duplicates that will be purchased for reserve (savings estimated at $4,000) and charges for photocopies will be increased to cover costs and overhead, which generates about $5,000 in new income. Nevertheless, these proposals merely represent a reduction of $24,000 in needed increases, plus a putative increase of $5,000 in income, leaving a shortfall of $107,000 if inflation were to be met.

As a second emergency step a permanent transfer of $20,000 from reserve is made to library materials to assist in maintaining periodical expenditure. At this stage no more can be done until all other budgetary reassessments are completed and a maintenance-of-effort deficit of $87,000 is recorded to be kept in mind as other areas of expenditure are inspected. No more than about $40,000 is, however, expected from any source.

(b) *Personnel.* Reduced intake of materials suggests that activity will be considerably lower, and that staff should be able to be reduced.

Using the activity indicators for technical operations, a new work-load distribution is postulated:

Number of books purchased	25,000
Number of associated activities	50,000
Number of serials parts	140,000
Number of associated activities	46,500
Number of other materials	180,000
Number of associated activities	90,000
TOTAL	531,500
Which is a reduction of	58,500

(a reduction of nearly 10 percent)

Similarly the number of catalog cards produced will be reduced but not in direct proportion since there is a time-lag. The likely reduction is from 530,000 to 500,000, or about 9 percent, unless further inroads are made on the backlog.

This projection suggests that vacant positions in the technical operations area can be collapsed and that reductions can be made in wages. The suggested figures are:

Full-time Personnel	$26,000
Wages	10,000
Total	$36,000

It is also possible that other staff reductions can be made if other suitable vacancies occur or transfers can be made. Technical Operations has therefore made, involuntarily, a substantial contribution to the imposed budget cut. In return other areas may be expected to provide help in maintaining the library materials program to the extent that that is possible.

(2) *Lending Services.* Despite the apparent slowdown in the actual circulation of materials, use in the library has increased sufficiently to require extra assistance in the stacks for reshelving. The need to undertake a major move of collections in the stacks over the summer also suggests that the usual lower level of activity cannot be counted on to enable extra work to be carried out during the rest of the year. Neither of the vacant positions can be spared, although one of them is redescribed from circulation itself to stack maintenance. In addition the reduction in reserve demands has released some time in photocopying and about $1,000 in wages will be released to help the stack maintenace section. It is, indeed, likely that some extra wage-help will still be needed.

(3) *Other areas.* The following brief summary sets out the results of analyses:

(a) *Personnel.* Both remaining vacant positions are collapsed, resulting in savings of: $30,000

Transfers are planned, as suitable vacancies occur, between Reference and General Services. The instructional program is reduced. It is also planned to leave some positions vacant for one or two months to generate savings.

The decision is made to reduce the wage budget by $50,000 (this includes the $10,000 from Technical Operations) and to rely on savings to enable the library adopt an operating budget of $220,000, which requires the use of $11,500 in savings. Net savings $50,000

(b) *Goods and Services.* Some standing expenditures are eliminated, *e.g.,* by reducing the number of telephones and reexamining all maintenance contracts. All items such as supplies are scrutinized for savings. The allocation for travel and research is reduced by $5,000. Some rentals for equipment are terminated. Not all these reductions can be realized, since in some areas inflation costs must continued to be paid.

However, the net savings is: $20,000

The summary of the results of the analysis thus far is:

(a) Reductions made to meet the University's goal of $71,180 (2 percent):

Full-time positions collapsed	$ 56,000
Reductions in Wages	50,000
TOTAL	$106,000

This leaves a surplus of $34,820 available for distribution for other purposes, which goes some distance toward meeting the inflation costs of library materials.

(b) Transfer of expenditures to meet library program goals (all these transfers are to the library materials budget):

From Reserve Funds	$20,000
From Personnel	34,820
From Goods and Services	20,000
From Added Income	5,000
TOTAL	$79,820

As a result the new library materials budget will be $1,140,320.

This is less than the budget required to cover inflation, which would be $1,193,025. The shortfall, which is $52,705, will be distributed: $20,000 to cancellation of subscriptions and $32,705 to Books.

It has now become very important to the library to have free disposition of all salary savings generated by the library. First call on these will be wages. The second most important distribution will be to goods and services, including travel and research. Finally, any surplus will be made available for library materials. The closest estimate is that savings may be in the vicinity of $50,000 for the year.

We now have the following historical record:

	Base Budget	1st Year Budget	2nd Year Budget
Personnel	$1,990,000	$2,224,000	$2,329,800
Library Materials	950,000	1,060,500	1,140,320
Goods and Services	200,000	209,500	189,500
Reserve	60,000	60,000	40,000
TOTAL	$3,200,000	$3,559,000	$3,699,620

This is, of course, the printed budget and includes extra income of $5,000 but does not show the reallocation of savings within the year's operation. The number of permanent positions has been reduced by 4 to 171 and wage help has been reduced by 5 FTE. The budget for library materials has been reduced significantly and certain categories of goods and services—e.g., equipment and travel—are almost entirely dependent on reallocated salary savings. It is significant that despite the reduction in programs the library is now paying considerably more for rather less, unit prices for people and things having risen. The library can make no further adjustment without eliminating programs, but consideration has to be given to finding substitutes for expensive labor, particularly in cataloging. The university's decision to maintain a 10 percent salary increase has meant that the average faculty member still does not understand the financial difficulties of the institution and expects the library to continue responding to his requests for materials and services.

Budgetary Actions: Third Year

This year the university can maintain the existing budget, but no allowance can be made for inflation. Salary increases will average 5 percent, but only on full-time positions. Adjustments to wages must be made internally. Any necessary changes can be made within the total budget structure, *but,* in addition, the administration guarantees a further $100,000 for library materials from institutional savings. No assurance can be given as to when this money will be made available, nor whether it can be continued to future years.

The same problems as before face the library. Price increases for library materials continue at the same rate. The security problem has become acute. There has been upward trends in reference questions and interlibrary loans, but a downward trend in reserves, while circulation and in-house use appear to have settled in a slightly lower ratio.

Studies carried out by the library staff have recommended two major changes. The first is the implementation of a security control system in the main library. The second is that the library participate in an automated shared cataloging system.

There are nine vacancies:

>One semiprofessional and one clerk in Administration
>One librarian in Acquisitions
>One librarian in Special Collections
>One librarian in Life Sciences
>One clerk in General Services
>One clerk in Reserve Services
>Two clerk-typists in Cataloging

The decision process follows much the same lines. Basic program commitments are made to:

(1) Maintain hours of opening, but not necessarily of all services.

(2) Maintain as far as possible the intake of library materials, giving preference, in this order, to serials, books, microforms, other materials.

(3) Implement decisions on automated cataloging, but at the same time to drop the present semiautomated ordering system, while keeping the batch-mode circulation system.

(4) Purchase the first component of a security system for the main library.

(5) Simplify the public service organization by amalgamating some functions, eliminating one special service and reducing specialists to half-time in their speciality.

(6) Require that Administration take the lead by reducing costs in that area.

In financial terms, the results of these program decisions are substantial. Without the guarantee from central administration of $100,000 for library materials, they would be impossible.

Library Materials

Initial examination of the effects of price increases reveals this situation:

	Present Budget	Cost Increases	Required Total
Books	$440,320	$44,032 (10%)	$484,352
Periodicals	647,000	97,050 (15%)	744,050
Binding	52,000	2,650 (5%)	55,650
TOTAL	$1,140,320	$144,732	$1,284,052

Of this cost increase the university has guaranteed $100,000, leaving a deficit of $44, 732. Only the most stringent economies elsewhere could provide such savings and it is therefore decided to provide only a further $10,000 by other economies. The final library materials budget, including the $100,000 guaranteed from the central administration, will be therefore be:

Books	$465,270
Periodicals	730,050
Binding	55,000
TOTAL	$1,250,320

New Library Programs

The cost of participating in an automated, shared-cataloging network will be $45,000 per year. This cost includes two terminals, maintenance and payments for cards. The elimination of automated ordering will reduce computer services costs by $10,000, but will require that a clerk-typist be added to the Acquisitions Department, and a filer be appointed.

The balance of new costs and savings appears to be in favor adopting the new program:

New Costs: Set up costs: Two terminals (purchased)			$7,000
Permanent costs: Maintenance			750
Charges for cards			17,500
Use charges, including line charges			26,750
Total cost for initial year			$52,000
Savings: Four clerk typists:	29,500		
Two semi-professionals	20,000		
Supplies (catalog cards, etc.)	8,000		
Other costs, maintenance, etc.	1,500	$59,000	
Computer service charges	10,000	10,000	
Total gross savings		69,000	
Less two clerks transferred to Acquisitions		10,000	
Total net savings		$59,000	
Favorable balance for initial year			$7,000
Favorable balance in subsequent years			$14,000

On the basis of the savings, the new program is incorporated into the planned budget for the year.

The cost of installing a detection system consists largely in the purchase of the detection device and the necessary labels. Subsequent costs for maintenance will be for labels and maintenance charges. In both cases, however, there will be a time cost for the insertion of labels. The set-up cost is estimated to be $21,000 and annual costs thereafter to be $5,750. The staff costs for initial labelling is estimated in the region of $10,000 and the annual cost to be $4,000, but this is mostly substitutionary since other ownership marking procedures will be eliminated. Despite the large initial outlay, the program is recommended because the annual loss rate, estimated to be about 4,000 books is actually costing the library $40,000 a year in wasted expenditures. The decision is made to draw on reserve funds on a temporary basis for the initial purchases, and to collapse one position to cover annual costs.

Summary of Changes

Not all the positions indicated above as candidates for collapsing are so collapsed. Instead a substitution in made in Special Collections where the vacant professional position is collapsed and one of the semiprofessional positions is transferred from Cataloging to Special Collections.

Sums Available for Reallocation from Internal Reductions in Programs.

The administration eliminates both vacant positions in its own area	$22,000
Two vacant clerk-typists positions in cataloging are eliminated	$19,500
Librarian in Special Collections is eliminated	$20,000
Clerk in Reserve Services is eliminated	$ 8,000
All other vacant positions are to be filled.	
Subtotal—sums from personnel-related expenses	$69,500
Reduced expenditures on supplies, etc.	$ 8,500
Reduced expenditures on computer services	$10,000
Total sum available for reallocation	$88,000
This amount will be rechanneled in accordance with the program decisions recorded above:	
Library Materials	$10,000
Goods and Services	$78,000

N.B.: The net growth for Goods and Services will only be *$59,500*, because $18,500 of the sum reallocated originally came from Goods and Services, albeit in different expenditure categories.

We now have a four-year historical record:

	Base Budget	1st Year Budget	2nd Year Budget	3rd Year Budget
Personnel	$1,990,000	$2,224,000	$2,329,800	$2,362,315[1]
Library Materials	950,000	$1,060,500	$1,140,320	1,150,320[2]
Goods and Services	200,000	209,500	189,500	249,000[3]
Reserve	60,000	60,000	40,000	40,000[3]
	$3,200,000	$2,559,000	$3,699,620	$3,801,635

Notes: (1) This represents the remaining full-time positions, to which a 5 percent salary increase figure is added, plus the same initial wage budget as for the previous year. In order to pay any rate increases to wage employees, either their numbers will have to be reduced or salary savings will have to be used, since no other budgetary provision is available.

(2) This figure does not include the $100,000 guarantee.

(3) An amount of $21,000 will be transferred temporarily from Reserve to Goods and Services to cover the set-up costs of the detection system.

The library has managed to accommodate a significant change in expenditure patterns within its existing budget. This was possible only because back-up savings were provided centrally for library materials. It is doubtful if the same process could be repeated. The number of full-time employees has now been reduced from a peak of 175 to 165. Despite central help the number of units of library materials acquired has been reduced yet again. All budgetary areas now rely heavily on the use of redirected savings or reserves.

Budgetary Action: Fourth Year

The financial squeeze has been eased slightly. There will be an increase of 1 percent available ($38,016), which must not be used for personnel. However, salary increases of 5 percent will be made, including wages. The $100,000 guarantee has been reduced to $75,000, but more might become available later in the year.

The background facts indicate some easing in problem areas. Some unease has grown concerning the capacity of the library to continue without the curtailment of programs, and this concern is particularly directed at the acquisition of library materials. Rigid control has for the last two years kept growth in serials numbers almost to zero. Both faculty and library staff have gone on record as saying that this has damaged the quality of the collections.

By now the automated shared cataloging system is working satisfactorily and reductions in professional staff can be contemplated.

Prices are increasing at the same rate.

The university in the last year reduced one or two programs in the humanities, but reductions in materials purchased have, as expected, increased the rate of interlibrary borrowing and the library is also lending more. The increases are on the order of 10 percent.

There has been a substantial change in use-patterns by the community; while a growth rate of 5 percent is being maintained, the emphasis has shifted from mornings to evenings.

The library was donated a substantial and valuable special collection and must provide housing.

The detection system is working properly and should be extended to cover more of the collection and one of the branch Libraries.

The reduced buying capacity has caused a reassessment of acquisitions programs, aggravated by the fact the librarians outside the Acquisitions Department have less time for selection because of increased reference needs; and the faculty, particularly in hard-pressed departments, are devoting less time to selection. Paradoxically it has been necessary to reduce the scope of "blanket" orders, which means that acquisitions "activities" have not been reduced. Strict control of new subscriptions is still being exercised.

There are five vacant positions:
One professional cataloger
One reference librarian
One clerk in accounts
One clerk in reserves
One clerk in lending services (Interlibrary Loan)

The most critical areas for maintenance of effort are in Library Materials and Goods and Services, where differential price increases have caused great pressures. The general staffing of public services presents problems that require long-term action, including a reorganization and some regulation of growth, which can, however, only be met by joint library-administration-faculty agreement. For the present, unavoidable needs must be met such as circulation and reserve services. Some control can be exercised by changing the hours when professional reference service is available and by policing the requests for interlibrary borrowing more strictly and passing on all costs to borrowers. Such measures are not popular and work only middling well, but progress is being made.

In this survey of budget action, the decisions taken will simply be outlined, with little discussion since the rationale remains the same.

Analysis

Library Materials.

The *operating* budget for the previous year was $1,250,320. Given the same rate of cost increases, the following infusion of finds is needed to maintain purchasing power:

	Present Budget	*Cost Increases*	*Required Total*
Books	$ 465,270	$ 46,527 (10%)	$ 511,797
Periodicals	730,050	109,507 (15%)	839,507
Binding	55,000	2,750 (5%)	57,750
	$1,250,320	$158,777	$1,409,154

To meet this requirement, the library has available:

Institutional budget	1,150,320
Library Savings	10,000
University savings	75,000
	1,235,320
Leaving a deficit of	173,734

Even with the most massive economies, the use of all the budget increase and perhaps the collapse of positions, it is impossible to find so much money. It is equally clear that Books cannot be expected to bear the whole brunt of inflation. Any further decision must therefor await examination of the remainder of the budget for possible sources of money, whether permanent or temporary.

Personnel.

Cataloging	The vacant professional position is collapsed:	$20,000
	A second position is transferred to Reference Services:	18,000
	Two clerk-typists are transferred, one to interlibrary loan:	8,000
	one to general services:	8,000
Serials	One clerk is transferred internally to periodical services	
	One clerk is transferred to lending services:	9,000
	One semiprofessional is transferred to Life Sciences:	12,000
Reference	The professional vacancy is filled at a beginning level, resulting in a savings of:	6,000
Administration	The accounts clerk position is collapsed:	8,000
Reserves	The vacant clerical position is collapsed:	9,000

General Services and Reference are amalgamated administratively. The actual savings generated total $43,000.

Goods and Services.

Operating costs for shared cataloging increase but the capital outlay for terminals is eliminated, resulting in a net reduction of $5,000.

Extension of the detection system will cost $5,000.

Price increases for mandated expenses will cost $10,000.

A decision has been made to eliminate subcatalogs, reducing equipment needs in this area, but not reducing on-going expenses by more than $1,000.

Telephone services are reduced and economies are effected by consolidating book lists, information memoranda, etc., resulting in a net saving of $6,000.

Travel and research expenditure and miscellaneous is reduced to a bare minimum, resulting in a saving of $10,000.
Net savings for other expenditures $7,000.

Summary

Increase in budget	$38,156
Salaries eliminated	43,000
Other savings	7,000
Total available for redistribution to library materials	88,158
Deficit on library materials	173,734
Net deficit remaining	$85,576

Examination of wage expenditure and expected salary savings indicates that most of the expected savings will be needed to maintain the present operating wage budget, with perhaps $20,000 available for materials as against $10,000 last year. The decision is made to reduce the wage budget by a further $30,000 and to put this amount into materials. Because even this action leaves a substantially lower budget for library materials, the processing staff can be reduced further. Three more positions from Technical Services are transferred to replace wage help in Public Service areas. *N.B.:* Not all these tranfers can be made immediately but are planned to take place through the year as vacancies occur.

The results of these changes in budget distribution are widespread. The acquisitions program has again been reduced. The most serious reductions have been for subscriptions which were decreased by 10 percent. All other reductions were turned over to this library program, together with a deep commitment from future savings. Public Service full-time staffs have been increased, but wage support has diminished. Specialized services have been restricted and organizational changes carried out to amalgate programs. During the year the library will continue to transfer positions as needed and possible. Maintenance has been reduced and other

APPENDIX *The State University Libraries: a Case Study* / **201**

Five-Year Budget Summary

	Base Budget	1st Year	2nd Year	3rd Year	4th Year
Personnel	$1,990,000	$2,224,000	$2,329,800	$2,362,315	$2,403,780[1]
Library Materials	950,000	1,060,500	1,140,320	1,150,320	1,268,476
Goods and Services	200,000	209,500	189,500	249,000	242,000
Reserve	60,000	60,000	40,000	40,000	40,000[2]
	$3,200,000	$3,559,000	$3,699,620	$3,801,635	$3,954,256[3]

Notes:

[1] Despite the higher total, the expenditure for personnel covers only 162 full-time positions and a loss of 4 FTE on wages, a net reduction of 7 FTE.

[2] Reserve funds will be required for the support of research and travel (now on a competitive basis) and for the purchase of equipment for extending the detection system.

[3] Three quarters of the entire increase is accounted for by raises in salaries. All the remaining new money went into library materials, together with all savings from any other area.

economies are being enforced. The library is in process of preparing a major position paper for consideration by Faculty and the Administration, pointing out the weaknesses that have developed and the high priority needs for financial relief. Initial contacts indicate a good reception in the administration but fiscal prospects continue uncertain. The framework survives but in a precarious balance. No one is happy; but, with varying degrees of understanding, the staff accepts the challenge to manage with reduced resources.

It is chastening to reflect on what has happened to the library programs over this five-year period. Despite the fact that the total budget has increased by $755,756, or 24 percent, the time and things purchased have decreased substantially.

Whereas the library began with 172 full-time staff members and 52.2 FTE on wages, it must now operate essentially the same programs with 162 full-time staff and 44.5 FTE on wages. In comparative terms, the library is now paying $415,280, 20.9 percent, more for 18 fewer FTE positions, a decrease of 8 percent. Apart from the reductions in cataloging which were in effect replaced by purchased services, there has been considerable reassignment of staff which resulted in a completely different distribution. The final comment required on personnel is that there is now considerable dependence on savings to maintain the operating wage budget, and the achievement of 44.5 FTE is in fact dependent on some savings from other vacant positions.

Other changes have been equally massive. The library Materials program has been curtailed and would be in even worse shape were it not for the reallocation of savings by the central administration. A comparison of initial and final distribution of both expenditure and expected product reveals the magnitude of the change:

	Base Budget	Units Purchased	4th Year Budget*	Units Purchased
Books	$450,000	45,000	$498,476	35,700
Periodicals	500,000	25,000	800,000	22,300

*Includes reallocated savings

Detailed changes in the allocation of expenditures for Library Materials would depend on immense numbers of individual program decisions over the years. The likeliest changes will be increases in the proportion expended on periodical subscriptions, and redistribution within that category of expenditure, where Sciences, Engineering and Life Sciences would undoubtedly now account for an overwhelming proportion of the total. The distribution for books would depend on whether the decision had been made to retain as far as possible an existing profile or to continue allowing such expenditures in the areas where periodical expenditure had increased most. In either case the discretion available is limited since only $11,476 more are being distributed than in the base year. All areas consequently will buy fewer books. A possible distribution is suggested in which the expenditures for general and special collections have been reduced, those for science and technology held down and any resulting extra funds diverted to the "book-dependent" arts, Social Sciences and Humanities. The result is a reduced program for the acquisition of library materials which has, nevertheless, sought to retain the same general shape. It recognizes the primacy of serials in scientific and technological areas but has not been able to offset the inflationary effects of prices in these areas.

Support expenditures are at a critically low level, which requires supplements from savings to maintain more than basic purchasing. Nevertheless significant changes have been accomplished, such as the introduction of a detection system and of shared cataloging. These new activities have caused a redistricution of costs that give the appearance of greater expenditure on goods and services until it is remembered that these are largely transfer costs instead of personnel who previously performed functions now contracted out. These new costs now carry with them their own imperatives and may be expected to continue influencing the shape of the budget.

It is difficult and probably not worthwhile to attempt to describe possible changes in services perfomed. Every attempt has been made to divert funds to critical public service areas and the staff has

Library Materials Distribution.

Area	Books	Periodicals	Binding	Total
Arts and Performing Arts	$ 27,000	$ 40,000	$ 3,500	$ 70,500
Humanities	53,000	80,000	7,000	140,000
Social Sciences	54,000	87,000	7,000	148,000
Languages	44,000	60,000	5,600	109,600
Education	11,000	16,000	1,200	28,200
Sciences	25,000	170,000	10,000	205,000
Engineering	20,000	105,000	5,700	130,700
Life Sciences	22,000	135,000	7,300	164,300
Reference	18,000	60,000	5,600	83,600
General	95,476	65,000	3,400	158,876
Reserves	22,000	1,000		23,000
Special Collections	20,000	6,000	700	26,700
	$411,476	$800,000	$57,000	$1,268,476

been augmented. Areas such as interlibrary loan will show a substantial increase in activity, as, to a lesser degree, will circulation. Some artifical control has kept reserve operations from expanding in order to provide support for reference services. In personal terms, most members of the staff probably feel they are working harder, particularly because it has been impossible to maintain faculty development support at the earlier level.

No doubt many alternative decisions might have been made, but the endeavor has been to construct a fairly likely scenario, which would illustrate the many kinds of decisions that must be made as a part of budgetary management.

APPENDIX *The State University Libraries: a Case Study* / **205**

Personnel Distribution (4th Year).

Department	Professionals	Semiprofessionals	Clerk	FTE Wages*
Administration	5	1	6	2.0
Acquisitions	3	3	10	3.0
Cataloging	9	3	14	1.5
Serials	3	1	13	5.0
Gen/Ref. Services	17	5	19	10.5
Lending Services	2	2	17	8.0
Reserve Services	2	1	4	6.5
Special Collections	1	2	2	1.5
Science	2	1	3	2.5
Engineering	1	1	2	2.0
Life Sciences	2	2	3	2.0
	47	22	93	44.5
Change from base year	(–3)	(–4)	(–3)	(–8.0)

*The operating wage budget is now dependent on the achievement of salary savings. It is not, therefore, possible to compare the personnel distribution expenditure by department including wages. If, however, they are excluded from both distributions, some idea can be gained both of the amount of redistribution that has occurred and the increase in the unit cost of labor. The reductions in technical services parallel the reductions in library materials purchased. Other changes attempt to reflect changes in work loads.

Personnel Expenditure Distribution.
(Full-time positions only)

Department	Base Year		4th Year	
	Number	Cost	Number	Cost
Administration	17	$174,000	12	$199,600
Acquisitions	15	147,000	16	160,200
Cataloging	36	380,000	26	379,900
Serials	21	185,000	17	205,000
Gen/Ref Services	37	403,000	41	583,500
Lending Services	19	159,000	21	228,000
Reserve Services	8	75,000	7	89,800
Special Collections	5	65,000	5	77,400
Science	6	65,000	6	86,600
Engineering	4	41,000	4	52,700
Life Sciences	6	62,000	7	95,400
	172	$1,755,000	162	$2,160,500

Glossary

Accrual Based Accounting   Under this system revenues are reported when they become due and expenditures are reported when they are incurred, regardless of whether receipt or payment is also made within the appropriate fiscal year.

Audit   The examination of documents, records of transactions, etc., which aims to determine whether proper procedures are being followed and whether the records accurately report the year's activities.

Budget   A statement that sets forth proposed income and expenditure for a stated period. Libraries are usually concerned mostly with the expenditure of funds.

Cash Based Accounting   Under this system only receipts and payments actually made during a fiscal period are assigned to that period.

Depreciation   In business this term covers the various accounting procedures used to amortize the cost of equipment over the period of its useful life. Most educational institutions do not provide specifically for this contingency by setting funds aside. Instead, plans are made to use a portion of the operating budget for the renewal of obsolete equipment.

Encumbrances   These are orders, contracts, etc., which represent obligations to pay at some future time. Another term frequently used is "commitments."

Endowments   These are normally special funds where only the annual income may be spent. Frequently the purpose of the expenditures is controlled by the terms of the endowment.

Fiscal Period   The period of time, usually a year, over which any given budget is operative.

Formula Budgets   These budgets make use of formulae, ratios, etc., for the computing of anticipated expenditure.

Incremental Budgets   These budgets "add on" sums of money for new needs in addition to those of the last fiscal period.

Line Item Budgets   These are the budgets commonly used for accounting control of expenditure. In them each line represents a different kind of expenditure. The numbers of categories may vary greatly.

Object Classification Budgets   These are similar to line item budgets but are usually more specific in describing the purpose of each segment of expenditure.

Performance Budgets   These are similar to program budgets and concentrate on the achievement of certain outputs.

Planning, Programming, Budgeting System (PPBS)   This is the name for an elaborate strategy which incorporates all three elements into the process of arriving at a budget. It was made popular by its adoption by the federal government. Elements within the system may be used: for example, the development of program measuring devices. Application of the entire strategy requires the analysis of all expenditures both direct and indirect and their appropriate application to programs of activities.

Program Budgets   These budgets usually group together all items of expenditure incurred in meeting the needs of a particular program. They emphasize inputs and outputs. A cross-walk is usually required for conversion into standard sets of accounts.

Restricted Funds   These are funds available to an institution but whose uses are controlled by an outside agency or agencies. A grant for the purchase of library materials on special subjects would be an appropriate example.

Workload Activity Indicators   A concept developed in PPBS, whereby statistical or other quantitative records are devised to measure work-load outputs, *e.g.*, student-credit hours.

Zero-Based Budgeting This method of budgeting assumes that each year budget requests are built up from zero in response to the priorities and needs of that year.

References

Allen, Kenneth S. (1972), *Current and Emerging Budgeting Techniques in Academic Libraries, including a Critique of the Model Budget Analysis Program of the State of Washington,* Seattle: the author.
American Library Association, Bookdealer Library Relations Committee (1973), *Guidelines for Handling Library Orders for In-Print Monographic Publications,* Chicago: American Library Association.
Association of Research Libraries (1975), *National Perspectives for ARL Libraries* (Minutes of the 86th Meeting), Washington, D.C.: ARL.
———. (1976), *Research Libraries and Cooperative Systems* (Minutes of the 88th Meeting), Washington, D.C.: ARL.
Axford, H. William, "An Approach to Performance Budgeting at The Florida Atlantic University Library," *College and Research Libraries,* 32:87–104.
———. "The Validity of Book Price Indexes for Budgetary Projections," *Library Resources and Technical Services,* 19:5–12.
Barnes, Frank (1971), "Budget Priorities for Libraries, " *Management in Libraries,* pp. 96–107 (edited by John Ponder), Melbourne: Ormond.
Baumol, William J. and Marcus, Matityahu (1973), *The Economics of Academic Libraries,* Washington, D.C.: American Council on Education.
"Book Price Indexes," *Library Resources and Technical Services,* 20:97–98.
Booz, Allen and Hamilton, Inc. (1970), *Problems in University Library Management,* Washington, D.C.: ARL.
Brazell, Jr., Troy V., "Comparative Analysis: A Minimum Music Materials Budget for the University Library," *College and Research Libraries,* 32:110–120.
Clapp, Werner W. and Jordan, Robert J., "Quantitative Criteria for Adequacy of Academic Library Collections," *College and Research Libraries,* 25:371–380.
College and University Business Administrations, Revised Ed. (1968), Washington, D.C.: Council on Education.
Cowle, S. R., "Presenting the Library Budget to the Appropriating Authorities," *Minnesota Libraries,* 22:329–334.

Cutt, James (1974), *A Planning, Programming and Budgeting Manual: Resource Allocation in Public Sector Economics,* New York: Praeger.

Davis, Otto A., Dempster, M. A. H. and Wildavsky, Aron, "A Theory of the Budget Process," *American Political Science Review,* 66:529–547.

Dix, William S., "The Financing of the Research Library," *College and Research Libraries,* 35:252–258.

———. (1972), "Reflections on Adversity; or, How Do You Cut a Library Budget?" (Eighteenth Library Lecture, Louisiana State University), *Library Lectures,* No. 17–20, pp. 8–18.

Dougherty, Richard M. and Heinritz, Fred J. (1966), *Scientific Management of Library Operations,* New York: Scarecrow.

Drake, Miriam A., "Forecasting Academic Library Growth," *College and Research Libraries,* 37:53–59.

Drucker, Peter F., "Managing the Public Service Institution," *College and Research Libraries,* 37:4–14.

Fairholm, Gilbert W., "Essentials of Library Manpower Budgeting," *College and Research Libraries,* 31:332–340.

Fazar, Willard (1968), *The Importance of PPB to Libraries: Paper Presented at an Institution on Program Planning and Budgeting Systems for Libraries at Wayne State University, Detroit, Michigan, Dept. of Library Science.* (ED 045 114).

———. "Program Planning and Budgeting Theory: Improved Library Effectiveness by Use of the Planning-Programming-Budgeting System," *Special Libraries,* 60:423–433.

Ford, Stephen (1973), *The Acquisition of Library Materials,* Chicago: American Library Association.

Galvin, Thomas J. (September 15, 1976), "Beyond Survival: Library Mangement for the Future," *Library Journal,* 101:1833–1835.

Gardner, Jeffrey J. and Wax, David M. (September 15, 1976), "Online Bibliographic Services," *Library Journal,* 101:1827–1832.

Gelfand, Morris A., "Budget Preparation and Presentation: Creating a Favorable Climate for Budget Approval," *American Libraries,* 3:496–500.

Goyal, S. K., "Allocation of Library Funds to Different Departments of a University—an Operational Research Approach," *College and Research Libraries,* 34:219–222.

Halstead, D. Kent (1975), *Higher Education Prices and Price Indexes,* Washington, D.C.: G.P.O.

Heinritz, Fred J., "Modern Scientific Management in the Academic Library," *Journal of Academic Librarianship,* 1:19–22.

Hirsch, Felix E., "Introduction: Why Do We Need Standards?" *Library Trends,* 21:159–163.

Institute on Library Management—PPBS, Eastern Michigan University, 1971 (1973), *Planning-Programming-Budgeting System (PPBS), Implications for Library Management* (edited by Lee, Sul H., Ann Arbor: Pierian Press.

Judy, Richard W. (1966), *Simulation and Rational Resource Allocation in Universities*, Toronto: Office of Institutional Research, University of Toronto.
Keller, John E., "Program Budgeting and Cost Benefit Analysis in Libraries," *College and Research Libraries*, 30:156–160.
Leimkuhler, F. E. and Cooper, M. D., "Cost Accounting and Analysis for University Libraries," *College and Research Libraries*, 32:449–464.
Lyden, Fremont James (October, 1975), "The Budget Cycle as a Basis for Decision Making in Higher Education," *Planning for Higher Education*.
Lyden, Fremont J. and Miller, Ernest G., editors (1965), *Planning Programming Budgeting: A Systems Approach to Management*, Chicago: Markham.
Lyle, G. R. (1974), *Administration of the College Library*, 4th edition, New York: Wilson.
McGrath, William E., "A Pragmatic Book Allocation Formula for Academic and Public Libraries with a Test of Its Effectiveness," *Library Resources and Technical Services*, 19:356–369.
McGrath, William E., Huntsinger, Ralph C. and Barker, Gary R., "An Allocation Formula Derived from a Factor Analysis of Academic Departments," *College and Research Libraries*, 30:51–62.
Marchant, Maurice P., "University Libraries as Economic Systems," *College and Research Libraries*, 36:449–457.
Massman, Virgil F. and Patterson, Kelly, "A Minimum Budget for Current Acquisitions," *College and Research Libraries*, 31:83–88.
Maynard, James (1971), *Some Microeconomies of Higher Education: Economies of Scale*, Lincoln: University of Nebraska Press.
Melcher, Daniel (1971), *Melcher on Acquisition*, Chicago: American Library Association.
Mortimer, Kenneth P. (1972), *Accountability in Higher Education*, Washington, D.C.: American Association for Higher Education.
Munn, Robert F., "The Bottomless Pit, or the Academic Library as Viewed from the Administration Building," *College and Research Libraries*, 29:51–54.
Natchez, Peter B. and Bupp, Irvin C., "Policy and Priority in The Budgetary Process," *American Political Science Review*, 67:951–963.
O'Neill, June (1971), *Resource Use in Higher Education: Trends in Output and Inputs, 1930 to 1967*, Berkeley: Carnegie Commission on Higher Education.
Parden, Robert J. (1970), *An Introduction to Program Planning, Budgeting and Evaluation for Colleges and Universities*, Santa Clara, California: University of Santa Clara, Office of Institutional Planning.
Pennsylvania State University, Office of Budget and Planning (1976), *Forms and Instructions for 1976–1977 Program Budget Planning*, University Park, Pa.
Pings, Vern M. and Spang, Lothar (1971), *Wayne State University Libraries Operations, A Description of Staff Deployment*, Detroit: Wayne State University.
Raffel, Jeffrey A., "From Economic to Political Analysis of Library Decision Making," *College and Research Libraries*, 35:412–423.

Raffel, Jeffrey A. and Shisko, Robert (1969), *Systematic Analysis of University Libraries: An Application of Cost-Benefit Analysis to the M.I.T Libraries,* Cambridge: The M.I.T. Press.
Richards, Jr., James H., "Academic Budgets and Their Administration—1962," *Library Trends,* 11:415–426.
Robins, Gerald B. (1973), *Understanding the College Budget,* Athens, Ga.: Institute of Higher Education, University of Georgia.
Rogers, Rutherford D. and Weber, David C. (1971), *University Library Administration,* New York: Wilson.
Rohlf, R. H., "Library Costs and Budgets," *Minnesota Libraries,* 24:39–45.
Schad, Jasper C., "Allocating Book Funds: Control or Planning," *College and Research Libraries,* 31:155–159.
Scheps, Clarence and Davidson, E. E. (1970), *Accounting for Colleges and Universities,* Revised Edition, Baton Rouge: Louisiana State University Press.
Schmidt, C. James, "Budget Recommendations for State-supported Senior College and University Libraries, 1968–1969," *Texas Library Journal,* 43:29–35.
———. "Resource Allocation in University Libraries," *Library Trends,* 23:643–648.
"Standards for College Libraries" (October, 1975), *College and Research Libraries News,* No. 9, pp. 277–279, 290–300.
"Summary of Major Findings, Conclusions and Alternatives, from the State Department of Finance Audit Division's Report on the University of California Libraries," *California Librarian,* 34 (i.e. 33): 18–22.
Summers, William, "A Change in Budgetary Thinking," *American Libraries,* 2:1174–1180.
Thomson, Sarah Katharine (1975), *Learning Resource Centers in Community Colleges: A Survey of Budgets and Services,* Chicago: American Library Association.
Wayne State University Libraries (1971), *Toward an Assessment of Academic Library Organization Effectiveness,* Detroit: Wayne State University.
Webster, Duane (1971), *Planning Aids for the University Library Director, Occasional Papers, No. 1,* Washington, D.C.: ARL.
Williams, Harry (1970), *Planning for Effective Resource Allocation in Universities,* Washington, D.C.: American Council on Education.
Young, Harold Chester (1976), *Planning, Programming, Budgeting Systems in Academic Libraries,* Detroit, Mich.: Gale.

Index

A

Academic profile of institution, 57, 114, 119

Academic programs: as budget factor, 26, 57, 115, 125; effects of changes in, 82–83; effects of new, 66–68, 103, 117

Accountability, 105, 139, 177; administrative, 22, 137; public, 3

Accounts, 13, 135; closing of, 169–170; monitoring of, 148

Acquisitions, 96, 113; accountability in, 149; current, 124–125; level of, 88, 98; patterns of, 88, 158, 173; in relation to academic programs, 84. *See also* Library Materials

Activities. *See* Workloads

Advance payments, 161–162, 169

Allocation of book funds, 113–133, 181; accounts in relation to, 126, 148; analysis of, 173; basis for, 114; between books and serials, 118; effects of inflation on, 120–122; institutional factors in, 116–118; library factors in, 118–119; standards for, 115

Analysis: financial, 5, 65, 171–174; political, 5; internal, by budget officer, 61

Audit, 107, 174, 177 n

Authority to expend funds, 145–150; centralization of, 21–22; distribution of, 147–148; on library materials, 156; limitations on, 39, 149

Automation: Effects of, 41, 130, 176

213

B

Book Budget. *See* Allocation of book funds; Library materials

Budget: analysis of, 31–32; definition of, 14; clarity in, 92; departures from, 30, 39; effect of fiscal climate on, 75–76; effect of uncertainty on, 146; format of, 8, 29–30; hearings 63, 95–97; reduced, 77, 113, 137, 139–142; request, 25–26; static, 76–77; structure, 31

Budget amendments, 162, 166 n, 167–169

Budget as communication, 95, 100, 142

Budget as control system, 6, 10, 20–21

Budget as planning document, 9, 15, 95, 142, 175

Budget as process, 8–9, 94–95, 139, 176

Budget as set of accounts, 8, 12, 93, 127–128, 135

Budget officer, advisory role of, 21, 60–61, 154–155, 160, 162

Budget presentation, 94–104; goal of, 94–96; use of alternatives in, 99–100, 103–104

Budget transfers, 7, 13–14, 18, 30, 133; between categories, 19, 30, 142; effect on program costs, 143. *See also* Budget amendments; Savings; Year-end funds

Buying power of funds, 84–86

C

Categories of expenditure, 54, 107, 171; interactions between, 26, 63, 90–91, 107

Change: as budget factor, 30, 95, 139; in plans, 168; in program needs, 105, 116; responsiveness to, 100, 143; in social environment, 137, 176; in technology, 129–130

Circulation, 56, 65–66, 97–98; constraints on, 81, 88; need to maintain, 77, 78

Collection development goals, 44, 88, 118. *See also* Library materials

Constraints: economic, 83–86; external, 16, 98, 103, 106, 143; institutional, 82–83; internal, 15, 80–82, 97; perceptual, 9–10, 94, 100

Consultation: within institution, 66; within library, 4, 22, 34, 58–61, 63–65, 175

Contingency planning, 168–169

Contracts for service, 31

Control, 12–13; definition of, 12; institutional, 17; limitations on, 97; location of, 147; purpose of, 21

Costs: of activities, 34, 53; of public services, 89–90; of transactions, 77, 89–90
Credit notes, 59–60, 165, 170
Cut-off dates for expenditure, 170–171

D

Decision-making, 3, 64, 97, 100, 142, 175; criteria, 63; dispersion of, 13, 21, 22, 137; fiscal considerations in, 19–20; program-related, 78–80, 133, 139. *See also* Authority; Control
Delivery schedules for equipment, 27, 148
Depreciation, 129–130

E

Effectiveness and efficiency as measures 72, 87–89, 173, 175, 177
Encumbrances, 119, 157–160, 173; year-end 120, 146, 169
Endowments. *See* Restricted funds
Equipment, 41–42, 130–131, 161; as capital expenditure, 42; replacement of, 130, 162
Estimates. *See* Projections
Expenditure, in relation to budget plans, 15–16, 150, 159–160, 171–172; on goods and services, 129–130, 162, 173; on library materials, 44, 78–80, 158–159; on personnel, 35–39, 105, 155–156
Expenditures, unavoidable, 12, 40, 43, 47

F

Feedback, 14, 165–166
Financial records, 4, 6, 12; check on correctness of, 30, 146–147, 150–151; need for accuracy in, 20, 21–22, 58, 131, 156
Fines, 45–46, 163
Fixed costs, 129
Flexibility, 18, 30, 123, 142, 167; institutional, 18; limitations on, 86; need for, 12–13, 126
Formula budget, 25, 50, 52, 57, 67, 101, 106
Fringe benefits, 112

G

Goals and objectives, 52, 65, 81, 95–98, 175; errors in setting, 68; institutional, 167; for library materials budget, 155; for personnel budget, 107–108; in relation to budget requests, 60–61
Goods and Services, 39–42, 130–133, 160–163; assigned to units, 40; classification of, 39–40; definition of, 31; effects of inflation on, 86, 161;

Goods and Services *(cont.)*
  encumbering, 160–161;
  neglect of, in standards,
  128; orders for, 162
Graduate assistantships, 33, 112

H
Hiring Expenses, 132–133

I
Income, 45–56, 162–164;
  estimating, 46, 59–60, 164;
  institutional 137–138; as
  related to budget, 45–46,
  59–60; sources of, 45,
  163–164; weakly related to
  expenditure, 137–138, 167
Incremental budgets, 64
Indexes. *See* Price Indexes
Indirect costs, 40, 112, 130
Inertia, definition of, 53; in a
  library system, 27, 76, 88,
  119–120, 176
Inflation, 26, 49–50, 77–80; in
  goods and services, 43, 161;
  in library materials, 83–85,
  120–122
Information, 49–61; categories,
  49–51; distribution of,
  46–48, 57; institutional, 57;
  management need for, 16,
  22, 34, 49–50, 165, 173;
  sources of 16, 28–30, 165;
  synthesis of, 10; use of, in
  budget preparation, 94–97
Instructions for budget
  preparation, 26; adherence
  to, 97; as control factor,
  91–92; nature of, 28–29
Interlibrary loan, 102;
  interaction with
  acquisitions, 69, 77, 80
Internal guidelines, 59–60
Investment: in academic
  program, 116–117; in the
  institution, 57; in library
  collections, 117–118; in
  library programs, 90
Invoices, 148–149; certification
  of, 156; foreign, 169–170

L
Legislation, federal, 109, 157;
  impact of, 111–112, 132;
  records relating to, 156
Library materials, 43–44,
  113–130, 156–160; as
  capital expenditure, 30;
  changes in distribution of,
  77–80; control of
  expenditures on, 149,
  159–160; cost of
  maintaining, 102;
  definition of, 31, 43; effects
  of inflation on, 84–85;
  support costs relating to,
  26–27, 78, 88–89. *See also*
  Acquisitions; Collection
  Development Goals; Serials

M
Maintenance of equipment, 31,
  41, 86, 130–131, 173

Marginal efficiency of investment, 87–88, 97
Measurement: of educational programs, 138; of library activities, 71–72, 87; of library materials budget, 44, 96; of library services, 89. *See also* Workloads
Minimum wage rates, 109, 143

N
Norms. *See* Standards

O
Object classification budget, 24, 106–107
Objectives. *See* Goals and Objectives
Order year, 158–159
Orders: control of, 21–22; timing of, 158–159, 161–162
Overhead, 54, 112

P
Part-time personnel, 33
Performance budget, 25, 50
Personnel, 33–39, 107–113, 147, 150–156; appointments, 152–154; categories, 33; changes in, 110; definitions, 31; development expenditure, 132; distribution of, costs, 34–35, 107–109; institutional expenditures on, 26, 75; overlaps in appointing, 153; records of, 150–151; reductions in, 113; in relationship to programs, 34; terminations, 151–152; turnover, 151
Planning, programming, budgeting system (PPBS), 16, 25, 50; effects on staff 64, 107
Prediction, 6, 69; difficulty of, 15, 72, 113–114; variability in, 122; of wages (as example) 37–39
Prepayments, 161
Price indexes, 83–84, 93 n
Priorities, 19–20, 86–90, 140–142; changes in, 77, 137; importance of, 19–20; institutional, 10, 91–92, 142; ranking of, 60, 68, 92–93; setting of, 86–87, 140; statement of 29–33
Program budget, 24, 34, 50, 68, 106, 126
Program-budget relationship in library, 10–13, 63, 99, 138–139
Projections: in budget development, 19, 69–71, 139; in library materials costs, 120–123; in personnel costs, 37–39, 155–156
Public services. *See* Services
Publications, sale of, 45

Q

Quantity and quality, 56, 66, 125, 129; as control factors, 97–98; need to be seen in context, 52, 71–72

R

Ratios, 52, 65, 90, 108
Reactive planning, 75–76, 167–168
Reallocation of resources, 20, 45, 67, 76, 82
Reductions in funding, 139–142
Reference activities, 71–72, 98–99
Rentals (of equipment), 41–42, 130–131; conversion of, 162–163
Reports, 165; interim, 166; Year-end, 171–174
Reserve funds, 44–45, 133–134, 154; purpose of, 45; use of, 119, 133
Restricted funds, 126–127

S

Salaries, 109–110, 151–155; correction of, 151; equitability in, 110, 153–154; increases, 110, 154–155; joint funding of, 112
Sale of library property, 45–46, 164–165
Savings, 167–168, 190–191; dangers of dependence on, 111, 124; institutional use of, 18; planning for, 123–124; records associated with, 133; use of, for acquisitions, 119; use of, for goods and services, 129; use of, for wages, 111. *See also* Year-end funds
Serials, 43, 88, 158; growth of, 118; increased costs of, 21, 78, 120–122; renewal of, 17
Service charges, 72, 77, 101–102, 143–144; philosophical considerations in, 89–90; response to, 80
Services: cost of, 89–90, 100; demand for, 97–98, 138; effects of increases, 119; expansion of, 76, 81; limitations on, 98–99
Standardization of data, 54
Standards, 6, 51, 74 n, 101, 107–108, 115; lack of, 72, 90; need for performance, 56, 96; use of, 73
Statistics, 16, 50–53, 56, 69, 100; comparative, 6, 51, 96, 101; as measures of activity, 50–51; problems with, 73–74; and standards, 51
Stockpiling, 130, 161
Student employees, 34, 111, 156
Student enrollment, 26, 57; and library materials allocations, 115; in relation to use of library, 29, 92

Subscriptions. *See* Serials
Substitutional costs, 53
Supplies, 41, 86, 130, 147–148, 162; records of use, 21; variability in need for, 31
Surplus and deficiency account, 46, 164

T
Tautness as administrative principle, 138–139
Technological impact, 7, 41, 129
Time as commodity, 31, 143
Transaction costs, comparative, 71
Transfers of funds between categories, 18, 20; year-end 169
Travel costs, 131
Trends, 16, 51, 139; analysis of, 71–73

U
Use of library as budget factor, 77, 88

V
Vacant positions, 35, 108, 151–152; effect of filling, on budget, 109–110; filling of, 152–154

Value *vs* cost, 90, 96

W
Wages, 33–34; controls on, 110–111; expenditure pattern of, 37–39; increases in, 155; records of, 155–156; use of savings for, 111
Weighting, in formulae and standards, 116–117
Working relationships, need for good, 16–19, 22 23 n; with administration, 16–17; with faculty, 64; with library staff, 64
Workload-activity indicators, 54–56, 69–72; as evidence, 99; as predictors, 108
Workloads, 50, 54, 97; in relationship to resources, 94–95
Work-study program, 111

Y
Year-end funds, 18, 117, 167–168. *See also* Savings

Z
Zero based budget, 106, 142